T0123483

MACAT

An Analysis of

Stephen Greenblatt's

Renaissance Self-Fashioning: From More to Shakespeare

Liam Haydon

Published by Macat International Ltd
24:13 Coda Centre, 189 Munster Road, London SW6 6AW.

Distributed exclusively by Routledge
2 Park Square, Milton Park, Abingdon, Oxon OX14 4RN
711 Third Avenue, New York, NY 10017, USA

Routledge is an imprint of the Taylor & Francis Group, an informa business

Copyright © 2017 by Macat International Ltd
Macat International has asserted its right under the Copyright, Designs and Patents Act
1988 to be identified as the copyright holder of this work.

www.macat.com
info@macat.com

Cataloguing in Publication Data
A catalogue record for this book is available from the British Library.
Library of Congress Cataloguing-in-Publication Data is available upon request.
Cover illustration: Kim Thompson

ISBN 978-1-912453-55-9 (hardback)
ISBN 978-1-912453-10-8 (paperback)
ISBN 978-1-912453-25-2 (e-book)

Notice

CONTENTS

THE MACAT LIBRARY

The Macat Library is a series of unique academic explorations of seminal works in the humanities and social sciences – books and papers that have had a significant and widely recognised impact on their disciplines. It has been created to serve as much more than just a summary of what lies between the covers of a great book. It illuminates and explores the influences on, ideas of, and impact of that book. Our goal is to offer a learning resource that encourages critical thinking and fosters a better, deeper understanding of important ideas.

Each publication is divided into three Sections: Influences, Ideas, and Impact. Each Section has four Modules. These explore every important facet of the work, and the responses to it.

This Section-Module structure makes a Macat Library book easy to use, but it has another important feature. Because each Macat book is written to the same format, it is possible (and encouraged!) to cross-reference multiple Macat books along the same lines of inquiry or research. This allows the reader to open up interesting interdisciplinary pathways.

To further aid your reading, lists of glossary terms and people mentioned are included at the end of this book (these are indicated by an asterisk [*] throughout) – as well as a list of works cited.

Macat has worked with the University of Cambridge to identify the elements of critical thinking and understand the ways in which six different skills combine to enable effective thinking.
Three allow us to fully understand a problem; three more give us the tools to solve it. Together, these six skills make up the **PACIER** model of critical thinking. They are:

ANALYSIS – understanding how an argument is built
EVALUATION – exploring the strengths and weaknesses of an argument
INTERPRETATION – understanding issues of meaning

CREATIVE THINKING – coming up with new ideas and fresh connections
PROBLEM-SOLVING – producing strong solutions
REASONING – creating strong arguments

To find out more, visit **WWW.MACAT.COM.**

CRITICAL THINKING AND *RENAISSANCE SELF-FASHIONING*

Primary critical thinking skill: CREATIVE THINKING
Secondary critical thinking skill: INTERPRETATION

The core idea of *Renaissance Self-Fashioning* is that the self (personal identity and ideology) is a more-or-less deliberate construction, in response to authorities such as the church or state. To demonstrate this, Greenblatt conducts a reading of major canonical texts to show the way in which the relationship of their authors to the power structures of their day was performed and represented within the text.

Consequently, writing (itself a construction of a type of self) becomes a way of understanding the self's subjection or resistance to authority, often in ways which are not apparent at the surface of the text. Instead, writing needs to be seen as a product of the whole culture that produced it, since it will have contradictions or unconscious references to a range of other texts, ideas, and concerns.

What makes *Renaissance Self-Fashioning* so successful is Greenblatt's ability to put sources together in unexpected ways, seeing deep connections between a range of source materials including plays, diaries, travel accounts, religious texts, letters, and reported speeches. In this way, Greenblatt bridges the traditional divide between literary and non-literary texts to demonstrate his hypothesis – that culture and history are deeply entwined and act upon each other in complex and subtle ways.

ABOUT THE AUTHOR OF THE ORIGINAL WORK

Stephen Greenblatt (b. 1943) is currently the Cogan University Professor of the Humanities at Harvard University. *Renaissance Self-Fashioning* established his reputation as a leading scholar of the Renaissance. He has subsequently written a number of books on William Shakespeare, including the bestselling 2004 biography *Will in the World*, as well as the Renaissance period more generally. He is a former president of the Modern Language Association of America, has held a number of major grants, and has won, among other prizes, the Pulitzer Prize (2012) and the Holberg Prize (2016).

ABOUT THE AUTHOR OF THE ANALYSIS

Liam Haydon was educated at Queen's University Belfast and the University of Manchester, where he wrote a PhD on Milton's *Paradise Lost*. He is currently a postdoctoral scholar at the Centre for the Political Economies of International Commerce at the University of Kent. His work focuses on the cultural history of the seventeenth century, exploring the connections between the corporation, economic ideology, and literature.

ABOUT MACAT

GREAT WORKS FOR CRITICAL THINKING

Macat is focused on making the ideas of the world's great thinkers accessible and comprehensible to everybody, everywhere, in ways that promote the development of enhanced critical thinking skills.

It works with leading academics from the world's top universities to produce new analyses that focus on the ideas and the impact of the most influential works ever written across a wide variety of academic disciplines. Each of the works that sit at the heart of its growing library is an enduring example of great thinking. But by setting them in context – and looking at the influences that shaped their authors, as well as the responses they provoked – Macat encourages readers to look at these classics and game-changers with fresh eyes. Readers learn to think, engage and challenge their ideas, rather than simply accepting them.

'Macat offers an amazing first-of-its-kind tool for interdisciplinary learning and research. Its focus on works that transformed their disciplines and its rigorous approach, drawing on the world's leading experts and educational institutions, opens up a world-class education to anyone.'

Andreas Schleicher
Director for Education and Skills, Organisation for Economic
Co-operation and Development

'Macat is taking on some of the major challenges in university education … They have drawn together a strong team of active academics who are producing teaching materials that are novel in the breadth of their approach.'

Prof Lord Broers,
former Vice-Chancellor of the University of Cambridge

'The Macat vision is exceptionally exciting. It focuses upon new modes of learning which analyse and explain seminal texts which have profoundly influenced world thinking and so social and economic development. It promotes the kind of critical thinking which is essential for any society and economy.
This is the learning of the future.'

Rt Hon Charles Clarke, former UK Secretary of State for Education

'The Macat analyses provide immediate access to the critical conversation surrounding the books that have shaped their respective discipline, which will make them an invaluable resource to all of those, students and teachers, working in the field.'

Professor William Tronzo, University of California at San Diego

WAYS IN TO THE TEXT

KEY POINTS

- Stephen Greenblatt is a literary and cultural critic, and *Renaissance Self-Fashioning* established his reputation.

- *Renaissance Self-Fashioning* argued that identity (in people and literature) was created by a response to state or cultural authority.

- *Renaissance Self-Fashioning* is a classic piece of Renaissance* scholarship, and the founding text of New Historicism.*

Who is Stephen Greenblatt?

Stephen Greenblatt is an American scholar, now based at Harvard, who was born in 1943 in Boston, Massachusetts. His father was a lawyer, and his mother was a housewife. He went to school at Yale and won a scholarship to take a year at Cambridge, before returning to pursue his graduate studies at Yale.

After he completed his PhD, Greenblatt took a position as an Assistant (later full) Professor at Berkeley, California, where he wrote *Renaissance Self-Fashioning*. At the time university campuses were hotbeds of radical politics, with protests against the established order of things. Greenblatt was influenced by these cultural and political theorists who were examining the way in which power operated in society, and the effect it had on the individual, and he began to realize that this could be seen in the sixteenth century as well as the twentieth. Much of Greenblatt's work has elements of autobiography, at least in the sense that it is often spurred by Greenblatt's own experiences (travelling on a plane, or the birth of his son). Greenblatt works these personal anecdotes into his scholarship to show how the past is at once more distant, yet also often much closer to our own lives, than it first appears.

Greenblatt remained at Berkeley until 1997, when he moved to Harvard. He is one of the foremost scholars of the Renaissance period, and of William Shakespeare* in particular, and has a won a number of major grants and prizes, including the 2012 Pulitzer Prize.* *Renaissance Self-Fashioning* established his reputation as an important critic, and he has continued to write about Shakespeare, sixteenth-century drama, and the Renaissance itself.

What does *Renaissance Self-Fashioning* say?

Renaissance Self-Fashioning considers the formation of identity in the sixteenth and seventeenth centuries, demonstrating that selves were formed (or "fashioned") in response to powerful social forces such as the church, state, or family. In fact, Greenblatt claimed that the same sort of process can be seen in the modern self, which is "fashioned" by similar responses to power as was the case 500 years ago. If any piece of literary criticism can be called "revolutionary," *Renaissance Self-Fashioning* certainly was – it emerged at a time of radical protest, and its ideas of repressive power and radical selfhood contributed to the clash between conservative and liberal values which took place in America from c.1960-1990.

Greenblatt argued that this process of identity formation can be perceived in literary texts, which reveal the structures of power in their society. He uses the tools of cultural anthropology,* psychoanalysis,* and history alongside literary criticism to unpack the concerns and anxieties of the society from which the text emerges. This insistence on reading the text as a product of its context was a marked departure from the prevailing mode of criticism, which saw the work of art as something divorced from its culture and politics.

Much of the context of the text was derived from the anecdote, often a private piece of writing or recollection of a particular conversation. These, Greenblatt argued, were insights into a culture precisely because they were so marginal – their authors or creators did not intend for them to be carefully crafted and measured, so they often revealed the unconscious thoughts and biases of a society. Placing these against more consciously constructed pieces of literature helped to reveal the ways in which the same anxieties and biases played out "under the surface" of Renaissance literature.

As well as its insights into the formation of identity, *Renaissance Self-Fashioning* offered a new way of reading literature. Starting from the idea that literary texts contain traces of the culture that produced them (sometimes in ways their author would not even have been aware of), Greenblatt demonstrated that it was possible to gain insights into that society from the literature it produced. How literature represented religion, shame, sexuality, or new peoples encountered overseas was indicative of the wider debates on those subjects. Consequently, the tensions and contradictions that a critic might find in a text would reveal the tensions also present in the society that produced it. Approaching a text in this way, and reading it in context with other, often non-literary, works allows Greenblatt (and the critics who follow him) the opportunity to see the orthodoxy and radicalism within society which writers of the sixteenth century would not have been able (or willing) to articulate directly.

Why does *Renaissance Self-Fashioning* matter?

Renaissance Self Fashioning was especially influential because it demonstrated the applicability of the ideas of Althusser* and Foucault* to the study of early modern* literature. Greenblatt was part of an interdisciplinary reading group at Berkeley that focused on the ways in which methodologies could be borrowed and recombined across disciplines; the group eventually founded a journal devoted to the topic, *Representations*, in 1983. Greenblatt's moving of these political theorists back to the early modern period perhaps stems from the emphasis this intellectual community placed on making connections between academic disciplines and modes of thought.

Renaissance Self-Fashioning is the founding text, and perhaps greatest achievement, of the school of thought known as New Historicism (or cultural poetics). It was a crucial driver in the shift from a criticism oriented entirely on the literary artefact to one that placed the text in its historical context, often in unexpected or even contradictory ways. Like *Renaissance Self-Fashioning* itself, New Historicism was not a prescriptive system of thought, but rather a way of questioning the boundaries in the past (what was permissible in a society, and who gave or withheld that permission, and how) and the present (New Historicism erodes the distinction between academic disciplines, as well as the objective boundary between the critic and their source materials that other schools of thought insist upon).

Not only is this a valuable text for those studying literature – especially, but not exclusively, Renaissance literature – it is an excellent example of a sustained theoretical reading of literature. Moreover, Greenblatt's arguments about identity, and the way we respond to social and cultural pressures, are as pressing now as they were when he was writing. Greenblatt has argued throughout his career that thinking about what is strange or striking about renaissance literature helps us to become aware the unconscious cultural biases that we ourselves have, and how they contribute to the power structures of our own time.

SECTION 1
INFLUENCES

THE AUTHOR AND THE HISTORICAL CONTEXT

KEY POINTS

- *Renaissance Self-Fashioning* was a major turning point in early modern literary criticism.

- Stephen Greenblatt's career at Cambridge and Berkeley exposed him to key thinkers who influenced his ideas on power and resistance.

- The text also emerges from the protests in 1970s America, making an exploration of the ways in which state power works more urgently.

Why Read This Text?

Renaissance Self-Fashioning was a startling intervention into the field of early modern literary criticism. It challenged one of the most influential approaches to literary studies – the argument that a work of art existed as a timeless artefact, separated from its environment – by demonstrating the cultural and political influences that the historical context had upon the literary text. *Renaissance Self-Fashioning* considers the ways in which the state (or other forms of power, such as society or the church) acts upon the individual, and whether the individual can resist the authoritarian* impulses of power.

These themes were not entirely new to critical thinking on the Renaissance, and were certainly present in the work of theorists like Foucault; however, Greenblatt's development of these ideas of power and the self through an extensive analysis of Renaissance literature and history was new and highly innovative.

> **"** A new kind of activity is gaining prominence in Renaissance studies: a sustained attempt to read literary texts of the English Renaissance in relationship to other aspects of the social formation in the sixteenth and early seventeenth centuries. **"**
>
> Jean E. Howard, "The New Historicism in Renaissance Studies"

The alternative methodology presented in *Renaissance Self-Fashioning* (now usually termed New Historicism, though Greenblatt initially preferred his own phrase "poetics of culture," which he saw as a more accurate description[1]) was remarkably influential. Greenblatt's mode of analysis quickly became one of the dominant forms of Renaissance literary criticism; in the words of a later scholar who has engaged with many aspects of New Historicism, Lisa Jardine,* "Greenblatt's book permanently changed the face of Renaissance studies."[2] *Renaissance Self-Fashioning* revolutionized Renaissance criticism, and scholars and students continue to engage with the themes, ideas, and methodology it puts forward.

Author's Life

Stephen Greenblatt was born in Boston, Massachusetts, in 1943. The ideas and figures discussed in *Renaissance Self-Fashioning* developed in stages throughout Greenblatt's higher education, which began at Yale University. Perhaps most importantly, after graduating from Yale in 1964, he won a Fulbright scholarship to Cambridge, where he first studied Renaissance literature as part of the graduate English program. During that time, he was able to attend lectures by the influential Marxist* critic Raymond Williams,* and began thinking about the way in which the political and cultural structure of a culture (or historical period) was reflected in its works of art. Some of these ideas were reflected in his graduate thesis, on the courtier,* poet, and

15

explorer Sir Walter Raleigh.* Greenblatt received his Ph.D. at Yale in 1969 before moving to the English department at the University of California, Berkeley.

He received tenure at Berkeley in 1980, the year *Renaissance Self-Fashioning* was published. As he notes in the updated preface to the re-issued *Renaissance Self-Fashioning*, this location was crucial because it introduced him to the prominent French philosopher Michel Foucault, who was a visiting professor in 1975. Foucault's work concerns the effect of society on the individual, and the ways in which those in power can coerce those they govern. His ideas profoundly influenced Greenblatt, who became increasingly interested in the way power functioned, not in modern society (Foucault's work does not often stretch further back than the nineteenth century), but in the Renaissance.

Greenblatt has continued to write prize-winning works (including the 2012 Pulitzer Prize) about the Renaissance, and in particular the work of William Shakespeare, and since 2000 has been the Cogan University Professor of the Humanities at Harvard University.

Author's Background

Renaissance Self-Fashioning emerged from a period of social and political upheaval in the United States. The 1970s saw a series of protests about the Vietnam War* and the resignation of President Richard Nixon* over accusations he had been secretly spying on his democratic opponents (the "Watergate Scandal"). There was, in Greenblatt's words, a sense that "everything seemed to be up for grabs."[3] In particular, the relationship between the individual and the various forms of power (state, media, religion, and so on) was being tested, and a number of alternative models seemed possible, ranging from the autocratic model epitomized by Nixon, to a freer society based on democratic engagement, protest, and individual liberties. In his early years at Berkeley Greenblatt distributed leaflets, went to mass rallies, and held teach ins against America's continued involvement in the Vietnam war.[4] This atmosphere of political instability, coupled with the repressive actions of American military power, clearly influenced *Renaissance Self-Fashioning*.

Though Greenblatt's work focuses on a period some 400 years earlier than its publication, its interest in the autonomy of the self in the face of church and state clearly resonated with 1970s America. Greenblatt himself commented on this link in a later, more reflective article, noting that "To study the culture of sixteenth-century England did not present itself as an escape from the turmoil of the present; it seemed rather an intervention, a mode of relation."[5] *Renaissance Self-Fashioning* argues that works of art are a key part of the power relations in a culture, and the questions it asks of the way in which power (and resistance) is voiced and represented emerge, at least in part, from the atmosphere of challenge, protest, and repression in which it was conceived.

NOTES

1 Stephen Greenblatt, *Renaissance Self-Fashioning* 2nd ed. (Chicago: University of Chicago Press, 2005), 5.

2 Lisa Jardine, "Strains of Renaissance Reading," *English Literary Renaissance,* 25 (1995): 291.

3 Greenblatt, *Renaissance Self-Fashioning*, xv.

4 Greenblatt, *Renaissance Self-Fashioning*, xv.

5 Stephen Greenblatt, "Resonance and Wonder," *Bulletin of the American Academy of Arts and Sciences* 43, no. 4: 16.

MODULE 2
ACADEMIC CONTEXT

KEY POINTS

- The New Criticism,* exemplified by Cleanth Brooks,* was the dominant mode of critical thought.

- Scholarship of Renaissance literature still focused on the text itself, particularly in relation to a long tradition of great writers.

- Greenblatt discussed culture as a whole by borrowing from a number of thinkers concerned with how power operated in a society.

The Work in its Context

While Greenblatt was writing *Renaissance Self-Fashioning,* Renaissance literary criticism was dominated by a movement known as the "New Criticism."

Though this was not the only way in which literature was read, it was nevertheless an influential critical approach, particularly in the classroom. The New Criticism asserted that a literary text should be examined on a purely formal and aesthetic level, as something that existed on its own terms, divorced from the context and politics of its production. This style of criticism was exemplified in the work of Cleanth Brooks, who warned that focusing on "what truth [poetry] gives, or about what formulations it illustrates" always came at the cost of finding "the essential core of the poem itself."[1] That core, he maintained, was found through a close study of the language of the poem, and nowhere else.

However, challenges to this methodology were emerging. The 1970s saw a number of studies that focused on contextualization over

> **❝** At the center of new historicism lies a claim that simply could not have been made in the United States twenty years ago with much safety or analytical rigor: that literature does political work. It does not rise above social life to a timeless aesthetic realm, nor does it simply reflect a coherent and hierarchical world view. **❞**
> James Holstun, "Ranting at the New Historicism"

the close reading of the New Critics, including literary criticism from Stephen Orgel,* and historical work on the politics of early modern literature from Christopher Hill,* though the methodology was not as prominent as it is now, nor did it have the theoretical impetus of Greenblatt's work.

Overview of the Field

The 1979 edition of *The Year's Work in English Studies*, a journal dedicated to providing an overview of the development of criticism in the field, reveals how dedicated the discipline was to the type of criticism suggested by Brookes. The article on Shakespeare, for example, has a series of studies dedicated to the internal coherence of Shakespeare's plays, with work on the connections between early and late plays, whether the endings problematically reverse the value judgements of the plays, and the strength of Shakespeare's narrative structures. There is also the question of "whether there is little new to be said about Shakespeare," and the suggestion that the best direction for novelty is in deeper appreciation of the dramatic progression within the plays themselves.[2]

Outside of Shakespeare, critics of Renaissance poetry still tended to follow the work of F. R. Leavis,* whose book *Revaluation* sketched out a line of influence from Shakespeare ("the pre-eminently ... English poet") and Spenser ("of the first importance in the tradition of English poetry") to Donne,* Milton, and then the Romantic* poets.[3] For Leavis, the work of the critic was to carefully tease out the ways in which writers assessed, borrowed from, and reinterpreted the great writers who had gone before them (and Leavis certainly demanded an assessment of "greatness" when performing criticism).

Leavis's work had been reassessed and updated by Harold Bloom* in his 1973 work *The Anxiety of Influence* that borrowed his conception of a line of influence but saw this as a much more problematic relationship, which included attempts at imitation and expansion, misreadings (deliberate or otherwise), complete reversals of style, and an overpowering of the poetic achievements of a predecessor. Like Leavis, though, Bloom was concerned with the development of great poets (and so his work naturally required value judgements to be made on what constituted "greatness"), and with a reading of literature in relation only to itself and other pieces of the great literary tradition.

Academic Influences

Greenblatt was profoundly influenced by the work of two cultural and political theorists, Louis Althusser and Michel Foucault. Greenblatt was part of an interdisciplinary reading group at Berkeley that focused on the ways in which these methodologies could be borrowed and recombined across disciplines. Althusser's work develops the work of Karl Marx,* arguing that the individual is formed by the actions of powerful agents of the state, such as the church, family, police, or education system (what Greenblatt calls "authorities"). In responding to these modes of power, Althusser argues, we learn through social convention to make ourselves into subjects: "the school ... teaches 'know-how', but in forms which ensure *subjection to the ruling ideology* or the mastery of its 'practice'."[4]

Foucault's work draws on the same Marxist tradition, and argues that the individual is actually created by the agencies that purportedly exist only to regulate that individual. In his book *Discipline and Punish*,

Foucault saw "punishment as a complex social function," and argued that the prison system has been used since the eighteenth century as a means of social control to create pliable, socially conditioned subjects.[5] Both of these thinkers are interested in the way ideological* forces determine the subject, and their influence can be seen in the central thesis of *Renaissance Self-Fashioning*, that selves in the sixteenth and seventeenth centuries were created in response to "authority." Greenblatt demonstrates the applicability of the ideas of Althusser and Foucault to the study of early modern literature.

NOTES

1   Cleanth Brooks, *The Well-Wrought Urn: Studies in the Structure of Poetry* (London: Methuen, 1968), 162-3.

2   David Daniell and Angus Easson, "Shakespeare," *The Year's Work in English Studies*, 58: 1, 1979, 127–171 (135).

3   F. R. Leavis, *Revaluation: Tradition & Development in English Poetry* (London: Chatto & Windus, 1936), 5.

4   Louis Althusser, "Ideology and Ideological State Apparatuses," in *The Anthropology of the State: A Reader*, ed. Aradhana Sharma and Akhil Gupta (Oxford: Blackwell, 2006), 88.

5   Michel Foucault, *Surveiller et Punir: Naissance de la Prison* (Discipline and Punish: The Birth of the Prison)., trans. Alan Sheridan (London: Penguin, 1991), 23.

MODULE 3
THE PROBLEM

KEY POINTS

- Greenblatt's work engages with questions of identity, politics, and culture that were being asked by historians and cultural theorists.

- Earlier literary critics had investigated the ideas of authority and resistance found in *Renaissance Self-Fashioning*, but without the same theoretical force as Greenblatt.

- Unlike those earlier critics, Greenblatt's work combines a number of disciplines to attempt a total view of the culture and politics of the Renaissance.

Core Question

Though *Renaissance Self-Fashioning* is now largely seen as an intervention into how we should read literature in its context, the core question in the text is one of identity and politics. Historians such as Christopher Hill and E. P Thompson* were stressing the need for a history of the early modern period which focused on "history from below;" that is, an emphasis on broad social movements and everyday lives. They saw identity and ideology as a product of culture (including literature) that developed organically, rather than being the imposition of "great men."

Literary critics, by contrast, continued to focus on canonical literature, which tended to be read either straightforwardly biographically or as self-contained pieces requiring no contextual exploration. Consequently, discussions over what identity was created through the text, or how it might be different from that of the author, was minimal.

> ❝ [I]n the sixteenth century there appears to be an increased self-consciousness about the fashioning of human identity as a manipulable, artful process. ❞
>
> Stephen Greenblatt, *Renaissance Self-Fashioning*

Greenblatt picks up on this idea to ask whether a self might be "fashioned" (that is, deliberately created) through writing. Is an identity something we can create for ourselves, or is it always created by, and in response to, powerful social forces such as the state, family, and religion? To answer this question, his book examines the social, cultural, political, and aesthetic structures of the Renaissance to assess how and why the people of the period had such a distinct sense of self. Greenblatt blends the tools of the historian, cultural anthropologist, and psychoanalyst to investigate what the Renaissance text can tell us about the power structures, ideologies, and structures of thought of the period. He argues that the process of forming identity within a literary text is broadly the same as the process in the "real world."

The Participants

Greenblatt's argument in *Renaissance Self-Fashioning*, that literature is a product of its social and political context and cannot be fully understood without understanding the structures of power with which it engages, was a direct challenge to the New Criticism. The polemical drive of Greenblatt's writing comes from his resistance to New Critical methodologies, a refusal to "wall off literary symbolism from the symbolic structures operative elsewhere" in society.[1] Though Greenblatt gave this argument particular force, the discipline itself was perhaps moving away from an emphasis on apolitical close reading.

As early as 1959, the literary critic C.L. Barber* had anticipated some of Greenblatt's arguments on "authority" (or power) and the way in which it seeks to contain subversion. Focusing on the work of the preeminent Renaissance dramatist William Shakespeare, Barber argued that his comic plays and characters dramatize "the anarchic potentialities of misrule";[2] that is, they are plays intimately concerned with the overturning of power structures. Though Barber's work sees this subversion as mainly limited to festive comedies, whereas Greenblatt sees it in all texts and at all levels of society, it is still a recognizable impulse towards the contextualization (and politicization) of the literary text.

The year before *Renaissance Self-Fashioning* was published, the critic and textual theorist Jerome McGann* made the argument that "poetic analysis *requires* an historical method if it is to achieve either precision or comprehensiveness."[3] Although McGann only saw history as a one-way effect upon the text (whereas Greenblatt saw the text as able to also exert an influence upon its context), their methodology for reading literature was quite similar.

The Contemporary Debate

In asking these questions *Renaissance Self-Fashioning* is in many ways a continuation of the work of the French philosopher Michel Foucault, especially *Discipline and Punish*.[4] In this book Foucault argued that punishment – and more importantly, the threat of future punishment through surveillance – was the way in which the ruling classes of a particular society produced docile subjects or workers. Greenblatt develops these ideas, questioning how far the self is "the product of a complex operation of power – of watching, training, correcting, questioning" or whether an individual can form his or her own self in relation to (rather than because of) power.[5] He also moves these questions back to the Renaissance, a period that Foucault does not consider (his historical work focuses on the eighteenth and nineteenth centuries). Until Greenblatt, these kinds of theoretical questions were rarely part of a discussion of Renaissance literature. *Renaissance Self-Fashioning* by contrast refuses to read texts as either the unique product of a brilliant mind, or as self-enclosed works to be studied solely on their own terms.

Instead, Greenblatt's project highlights key historical and social developments in defining identity, not least the clash between religious ideas of selfhood (a created self) and those of the humanists,* who argued that mankind was responsible for their own improvement through learning and experimentation. However, this question – what makes a "self"? – is as important a question now as it was in the sixteenth and seventeenth centuries. The questions that *Renaissance Self-Fashioning* raises about how we respond to power, and whether there is such thing as the "individual," remain pressing concerns of modernity and postmodernity.*

NOTES

1   Stephen Greenblatt, *Renaissance Self-Fashioning* 2nd ed. (Chicago: University of Chicago Press, 2005), 3.

2   C.L. Barber, *Shakespeare's Festive Comedy: A Study of Dramatic Form and its Relation to Social Custom* (Princeton, NJ: Princeton University Press, 2012 [1959]), 13.

3   Jerome McGann, "Keats and the Historical Method in Literary Criticism," *Modern Language Notes* 94, no. 5: 1000.

4   Michel Foucault, *Surveiller et Punir: Naissance de la Prison* (Discipline and Punish: The Birth of the Prison)., trans. Alan Sheridan (London: Penguin, 1991).

5   Greenblatt, *Renaissance Self-Fashioning*, 80.

THE AUTHOR'S CONTRIBUTION

KEY POINTS

- Greenblatt argues that there was a shift in how identity was created in the sixteenth century.

- In a series of case studies, Greenblatt shows how this creation happened: by submission or resistance to a range of authorities.

- Greenblatt's methodology draws from a range of different theorists, but is closest in practice to the "thick description" of Clifford Geertz.*

Author's Aims

Greenblatt sets out his aims clearly in the first sentence of the book, claiming that "in sixteenth century England there were both selves and a sense they could be fashioned."[1] By this he means that the early modern period was a break from previous types of identity formation, which he saw as being more or less imposed on the populace. He aimed to show in *Renaissance Self-Fashioning* that in this period individuals began to have agency around how they interacted with authorities such as church or state; as a consequence, their selves were no longer imposed, but fashioned.

In some ways, the work is a development of Greenblatt's first book, *Sir Walter Raleigh: The Renaissance Man and His Roles*.[2] Here, he focused on the courtier and explorer Raleigh as an individual, arguing that at key moments in his life and career he was engaged in a theatrical performance, designed to alter the way he was perceived by society at large. In its consistent interrogation of play, performance, and improvisation, *Renaissance Self-Fashioning* picks up on these early ideas;

> **❝** I believed that in describing some of the models of identity formation in the Renaissance I was participating, in a small, scholarly way, in a much larger project, the project of grasping how we have become the way we are. **❞**
>
> Stephen Greenblatt, *Renaissance Self-Fashioning*

however, the later work is less secure in its identification of agency entirely with the individual, preferring to see the "self" not as an individual performance but as a response to social and cultural pressures.

This thesis required a new way of thinking about literature. *Renaissance Self-Fashioning* places the work of art into a series of (sometimes surprising) political, historical, social, and religious contexts, to show the ways in which traces of those authorities found their way into the literary productions of the authors he studies. Thinking about culture and society as a series of continuous interactions was a challenge to prevailing orthodoxies that focused almost exclusively on the text itself, and read it only in relation to other literature, not its historical context.

Approach

Renaissance Self-Fashioning places the literary works of prominent authors alongside their historical context to show how ideas and beliefs are spread, and how the writers react to them to fashion their identities. It relies on six individual case studies to make its argument about identity. These case studies can be divided into two broad themes, with the first three considering the authority of the church, and the second three the state. There is, therefore, a consistent thread running through the book, as Greenblatt examines the way individuals submit to, or rebel against, established modes of power. Each of these case studies is illuminated through a number of related contextual themes: the discourse of colonial power, the Reformation,* the rise in printing, and varied and conflicting ideas of sexuality.

Though Greenblatt was not the first critic to think about texts contextually, he was unique in the way he mixed disciplines and ideas: rather than offering a psychoanalytic, religious, or colonial reading of a text, he aimed to show how those ideas integrated in the identity of the writers and were then refracted in their writings. Moreover, he showed that culture was not something simply happening to the literary text, but rather the literary text was a crucial part of the construction of culture – for instance, the image of Elizabeth I, an imposing authority, was itself created through the sort of fictions and representations that Greenblatt analyzes.

Contribution in Context

Greenblatt's methodology borrows heavily from the anthropologist Clifford Geertz, whose model of "thick description" was a key influence on Greenblatt. Geertz's work takes a single, often personal, anecdote, and builds from that into a description of an entire culture – most famously, his experience of a cock-fight in Bali is used to discuss the "connection between the excitements of collective life and those of blood sport."[3] The crowd Geertz observes at the cock-fight leads him to a discussion of the broader social phenomenon of the local people, such as their relationship to authority, kinship, and gambling that in turn leads to a discussion of pride and masculinity, so that the cockfight "provides a metasocial commentary upon the whole matter of assorting human beings."[4] *Renaissance Self-Fashioning*, too, attempts to analyze the whole field of culture, though rather than the gesture or event, it takes as the starting point for its description the act of writing.

Greenblatt's focus on the social pressures, and the cultural conditions of the self, heralded a marked change in practice from existing critical approaches to early modern literature (which had often focused exclusively on the text itself). The radical elements of the text – the questioning of dominant power structures, and in particular the power of culture to subvert or destroy those structures – placed *Renaissance Self-Fashioning* at the forefront of the newly politically aware movement within literary criticism. Moreover, the mix of methodologies that Greenblatt deploys in the text – textual analysis, historical context, cultural anthropology, political theory, and psychoanalysis demonstrated the richness of the cultural artefact, and the range of intellectual tools needed to examine it fully. By cutting across these different disciplines, *Renaissance Self-Fashioning* joined thinkers like Foucault in opening up a new intellectual framework for English literature.

NOTES

1   Stephen Greenblatt, *Renaissance Self-Fashioning* 2nd ed. (Chicago: University of Chicago Press, 2005), 1.

2   Stephen Greenblatt, *Sir Walter Ralegh: The Renaissance Man and His Roles* (New Haven and London: Yale University Press, 1973).

3   Clifford Geertz, "Notes on the Balinese Cockfight" in *The Interpretation of Cultures* (NY: Basic Books, 2000 [1973]), 425.

4   Geertz, 448.

SECTION 2
IDEAS

MAIN IDEAS

KEY POINTS

- Greenblatt sees the self as an identity created in response to authority.

- There is no singular "authority," and Greenblatt shows how different individuals respond to different authorities, sometimes in contradictory ways.

- The text is an approachable digest of ideas and literatures, though it can be Anglocentric* at times.

Key Themes

The central theme of *Renaissance Self-Fashioning* is that the self is created by a submission to authority and a rejection of an "alien," a force outside of, or oppositional to, that authority. These authorities and aliens take different forms for different cultures, and for different people within different cultures, and so the book is ordered around six case studies – More,* Tyndale,* Wyatt,* Spenser,* Marlowe,* and Shakespeare – each of whom responds to a specific type of authority and alien. The first three figures are read alongside their literary works, to consider how their biographies and their writings interact. The second three are read as the product of a later period that saw writing as a career; that is, when being a "writer" became an identity in itself. As a result, Greenblatt finds in their writing "complex and seemingly autonomous characters in fully realized fictional worlds,"[1] and so focuses on the writing more than the biographies of the writers.

Though this structure may seem to be a succession of anecdotal histories, or discrete sets of analysis, each of these figures is seen as placed within a larger pattern. All of these individuals are seen to have

> 66 There is no such thing as a single 'history of the self' in the sixteenth century, except as the product of our own need to reduce the intricacies of complex and creative beings to safe and controllable order. 99

Stephen Greenblatt, *Renaissance Self-Fashioning*

powerful anxieties about the authorities to which they submit, and the effects of that submission, which are transmitted in their writings. Through these examples, a fuller "poetics of culture" can be glimpsed, providing a sense of the anxieties and oppositions self-fashioning produced for those within the Renaissance (and beyond).[2] The question of response to an authority is one of the most commonly debated of all the issues Greenblatt raises, since it opens two possibilities of subjectivity: one determined by free will and the individual, one determined by powerful forces outside of that individual's control or influence. As Greenblatt notes in his epilogue, though his figures have "traces of free choice," that choice is nonetheless "among possibilities whose range was strictly delineated by the social and ideological system in force."[3] Any reading of *Renaissance Self-Fashioning* is likely to raise questions about how far an individual is able to fashion themselves (if at all), and how far they are fashioned from outside.

Exploring the Ideas

The central theme of *Renaissance Self-Fashioning*, that identity is created in response to social and cultural pressure, runs through every chapter, and should be seen as the most important idea it presents. This idea, though, is developed by Greenblatt in a number of ways, which sometimes seem contradictory. The first half of the book is concerned with responses to religious authority, and the anxieties that change in religious systems produced in the writers Greenblatt studies. The first chapter, on the Lord Chancellor and Catholic martyr

Sir Thomas More, shows identity being formed through the submission to the social codes and practices instituted (at least in part) by the Catholic Church; truth, in Greenblatt's reading of More, is found in tradition and "communal consciousness."[4] Yet the reverse is also true, since Greenblatt finds in the Protestant preacher and martyr William Tyndale a rejection of social authority in favor of the "individual" and his "own conscience," as well as the power of the printed book.[5]

The second half of the book produces similarly oppositional themes, though here the focus is the secular power of Elizabeth and the state, not specifically the Church. Greenblatt's analysis of Spenser's epic poem *The Faerie Queene* argues that it functions in a similar manner to More's writing. Spenser's poem marks a complete submission to Elizabeth (represented allegorically in the poem as Gloriana, the Faerie Queen herself), creating a "coherent, stable identity anchored in the ardent worship of power."[6] Here, again, Greenblatt immediately provides the opposition to his analysis, finding in the dramatist Christopher Marlowe an unrelenting drive to "spurn and subvert his culture's metaphysical and ethical certainties," such as his depiction of cruel yet seductive power in *Tamburlaine* (c.1587).[7] For both halves of the book, there are summary chapters (chapter 3 on the poet Thomas Wyatt, and chapter 6 on the dramatist William Shakespeare) that bring together the conflicting themes of the earlier chapters.

These examples demonstrate the point that Greenblatt makes in the introduction, that "one man's authority is another man's alien."[8] That is, there is no single point of authority (and no single "alien," or opposition to that authority), but rather a whole series of competing institutions; individuals can and do respond to these authorities in very different ways. *Renaissance Self-Fashioning* can thus be read as a whole work that engages broadly with the development of a sense of identity in the Renaissance or as a series of discrete essays on prominent

Renaissance figures. However, it is important to see that the themes Greenblatt sketches are dialectic* (or oppositional); by placing them side-by-side, Greenblatt suggests that identity is not formed by a monolithic authority, but is rather a variable process dependent on what authorities (and aliens) an individual recognizes and responds to.

Language and Expression

Greenblatt's varied source texts and sophisticated theoretical language can be challenging for new students of the period. Much of his work draws together fragments of obscure texts, which are apparently unrelated, in order to demonstrate an underlying theme or idea, and this can be difficult to follow for students (and scholars) unfamiliar with the range of literary and historical texts that Greenblatt cites. Nonetheless, Greenblatt's own style is engaging and approachable, and building his larger ideas out from small anecdotes (a dinner party, a single encounter in Sierra Leone) allows the reader to follow his thought process. Moreover, although he borrows their ideas, he rarely adopts wholesale the intimidating language of philosophers and theorists such as Foucault and Lacan.*

Greenblatt assumes, however, that his readership sits securely within the English-speaking, Western (or even North American) academic community. His methodology relies on placing the literary text within a social and cultural history. However, the choice of contexts for the literary text is already an interpretative choice, since his "contextualization is just another form of interpretation, another way of deciding where and how to center the competing claims made on our attention by a variety of needs and desires."[9] By placing Spenser's epic *The Faerie Queene* alongside narratives of English colonialism in the New World and Ireland, as he does in Chapter Four, Greenblatt privileges the writings of the colonizing or oppressive forces at the expense of all other potential histories.

NOTES

1   Stephen Greenblatt, *Renaissance Self-Fashioning* 2nd ed. (Chicago: University of Chicago Press, 2005), 161.

2   Greenblatt, *Renaissance Self-Fashioning*, 5.

3   Greenblatt, *Renaissance Self-Fashioning*, 256.

4   Greenblatt, *Renaissance Self-Fashioning*, 53.

5   Greenblatt, *Renaissance Self-Fashioning*, 99.

6   Greenblatt, *Renaissance Self-Fashioning*, 179.

7   Greenblatt, *Renaissance Self-Fashioning*, 220.

8   Greenblatt, *Renaissance Self-Fashioning*, 9.

9   Edward Pechter, "The New Historicism and Its Discontents: Politicizing Renaissance Drama," *PMLA* 102 (1987): 298.

MODULE 6
SECONDARY IDEAS

KEY POINTS

- As well as the major figures of authority in church and state, Greenblatt records a series of other important influences on self-fashioning.

- Individuals can subject themselves to more than one authority at once, but this creates intellectual tensions.

- Though the work has been thoroughly responded to, the psychoanalytic elements are those which have been picked up least.

Other Ideas

Renaissance Self-Fashioning argues that identity is created in the meeting between powerful social forces and the agency of the individual. It demonstrates this primarily by looking at two of the most powerful social structures in Renaissance England: the Bible and the monarch. The main focus of the book thus has potentially broad applications (though it is itself based on specific examples), since all citizens of Renaissance England, it might be argued, had to respond in some way to the ideologies of church and state. However, Greenblatt also offers a number of other authorities at a local or individual level that demonstrate the way power works through interlinked institutions or ideologies.

The two most important additional authorities in the book are the practice of colonization, and the idea of community. Greenblatt shows how the epic poet Spenser was influenced by the ideas of conquest and colonization he encountered while in Ireland (that was at this time under English rule). These ideas play out in an anxious

> ❝ Questions about authorial self-representation and the nature of the book become questions about the status of representation within the book, the nature of characters as voices for the poet and representations of the act of authoring. ❞
>
> Jonathan Goldberg, *Voice Terminal Echo*

nationalism* within Spenser's epic *The Faerie Queene*, in particular the acts of creation-through-destruction it records, and in the distant figure of Elizabeth.

As well as the specific instances of community-thinking given in the text – such as national identity, or the concept of social shame – Greenblatt's work demonstrates the way in which being part of an intellectual or social community shapes a work of culture. These ideas – that there are local power structures that affect self-fashioning, and self-fashioning takes place through language – deepen and enrich Greenblatt's central thesis, demonstrating the nuances and complications of self-fashioning that would not be visible at the broad level of church and state.

Exploring the Ideas

As well as Spenser's role in Ireland, Greenblatt also discusses the sixteenth-century Spanish conquest of the New World (the Americas). This, like the English experience in Ireland, offers a chance for Renaissance writers and thinkers to reflect on their own culture through its contact with an "Other." Greenblatt argues that the actions which these colonizers take (often spontaneously, in a mode he calls "improvisation") in order to coerce the natives, unconsciously reveal the way they think about their own culture; indeed, it would never be possible to reflect on their own culture in such a fashion without an "Other" onto whom they project their deepest fears and anxieties.

Likewise, when discussing Sir Thomas More, Greenblatt argues that although the Bible is a key authority, More was primarily interested in the idea of community. In the first chapter of *Renaissance Self-Fashioning*, Greenblatt argues that More's writing always involves the individual submitting to the needs of the community, so that the self is absorbed into the greater good: "He wishes to cancel his own identity,"[1] though this cancellation is never entirely achieved. Although this is primarily a response to a religious community, we can see that the *idea* of the community exists for More in a number of different forms. Thus, from the very start of the book Greenblatt is able to demonstrate the different, yet interlinked, sets of authorities on which self-fashioning depends.

Greenblatt claims in the introduction that "There is always more than one authority and more than one alien [that which resists or opposes authority] in existence at a given time."[2] Although *Renaissance Self-Fashioning* does consider a number of different authorities in each chapter, these are largely shown to appear different but actually to be the same – so the chapter on *Othello* considers state power that is both generous and destructive alongside the actions of the Spanish colonists in the Americas, which rely on persuading, rather than forcing, the natives to follow orders. These are both seen as symptoms of the power of improvisation, the ability to use and repurpose existing materials and beliefs to create order. This opens the possibility, not discussed in *Renaissance Self-Fashioning*, that different authorities will work in conflicting or contradictory ways on the individual; or, at least, that we might be able to perceive the tensions created by this conflict within the texts we analyze. This would enrich our understanding of the way subjects fashion their own identity, as well as giving a better sense of how authorities interact with one another.

Overlooked

Greenblatt's work has been prominent for a long time, and so *Renaissance Self-Fashioning* has been used, repurposed, and criticized quite fully. However, a relatively overlooked element of his methodology is the use of psychoanalysis; the focus on history and context from those following Greenblatt has meant that the psychology of the individual author (or character) is seen as less important than the broad trends or ideas with which the text engages.

In his discussion of the William Shakespeare's play *Othello* (c.1603), Greenblatt uses the psychoanalytical critic Lacan to think about the way the title character constructs himself in language. Greenblatt finds in Othello the "dependence of even the innermost self on a language that is always necessarily given from without,"[3] and argues that all theatrical identity is constructed in this manner. This, then, is an intervention into both the general idea of self-fashioning, the ability to construct a self through language or narrative, as well as the specific circumstances of the theatre. By using this analytical model, Greenblatt shows that the conditions of the theater (in which an actor speaks the lines a playwright has written) are reproduced in the identity of the characters themselves. The theater is therefore a double performance – an actor and a character both performing an identity that is not entirely theirs – and this changes how we might analyze the dramatic text both on the page and the stage, with a renewed focus on the psychology of the individual and how they represent themselves (and are represented). There are some critics, such as Jonathan Goldberg,* who combine these insights with historicist enquiry, but the psychoanalytical method he uses in *Renaissance Self-Fashioning* has not been generally or consistently incorporated into historical criticism.[4]

NOTES

1   Stephen Greenblatt, *Renaissance Self-Fashioning* 2nd ed. (Chicago: University of Chicago Press, 2005), 54.

2   Greenblatt, *Renaissance Self-Fashioning*, 9.

3   Greenblatt, *Renaissance Self-Fashioning*, 245.

4   Jonathan Goldberg, *Voice Terminal Echo* (New York: Methuen, 1986).

MODULE 7
ACHIEVEMENT

KEY POINTS

- *Renaissance Self-Fashioning* was immediately acknowledged as a crucial intervention in Renaissance literary studies.

- Greenblatt's methodology has gained some traction outside of the Renaissance, with scholars of the Medieval* and Romantic periods.

- Greenblatt has been criticized for drawing his evidence primarily from a white, male, middle-class, European culture.

Assessing the Argument

Greenblatt acknowledges, in the retrospective preface attached to the reissue of *Renaissance Self-Fashioning*, that the book was not intended to be a "master narrative" for Renaissance literature, but instead "came about in a rather haphazard way."[1] In a sense, though, that "haphazard" mode of construction actually adds to the text, as a further demonstration of Greenblatt's arguments for the deep relationships between forms of culture and political ideas; having such a wide variety of sources in discussion actually helps to demonstrate the totality of culture for which Greenblatt is arguing.

Despite this somewhat piecemeal methodology, *Renaissance Self-Fashioning* achieves its intent of bringing the concept of self, and the construction of the self, to the forefront of literary study. All identity, Greenblatt intended to argue, was in some way a self-conscious performance; however, *Renaissance Self-Fashioning* does not quite reach such a confident assertion of individual agency. Greenblatt finds in all

> ❝ The importance of Stephen Greenblatt's *Renaissance Self-Fashioning* as an intervention in Renaissance Studies is incontestable – he altered forever not just the field, but the manner in which it was studied [even where subsequent work was purportedly oppositional to him]. ❞
>
> Lisa Jardine, "Strains of Renaissance Reading"

the figures he discusses a submission to authority, a constant surrendering of agency to significant structures of power such as the church, state, or family. These sites of power act upon the individual, but Greenblatt's individuals do not have an equal capacity to alter the forms of power that fashion their identities (though they maintain the will to do so). Greenblatt does not necessarily see this as a bleak or pessimistic conclusion, preferring instead to emphasize the general trend of resistance to power, but the book is ultimately less optimistic than Greenblatt's earlier work.

Achievement in Context

Renaissance Self-Fashioning was almost immediately regarded as an important and influential work; it is now accepted as the founding document of New Historicism, a school of thought that embraces Greenblatt's desire to see the literary text not as an isolated artefact, but as part of a historical and political context. New Historicism, despite its profound influence on early modern studies, has not been adopted as a standard methodology outside of that time period. This is possibly because the early modern period provides a particularly apt model for the arguments that Greenblatt is making: "there is in the early modern period a change in the intellectual, social, psychological, and aesthetic structures that govern the generation of identities."[2]

Although there have been, of course, scholars from a range of historical periods who have used Greenblatt's work (particularly medieval scholars pushing his work back before 1500), the only other movement to have a sustained engagement with Greenblatt's methodology is Romanticism, spanning the late eighteenth to early nineteenth century. In many ways, these additional lines of historical enquiry were developed independently of Greenblatt's particular work, which is rarely discussed in these texts. They are, however, certainly indebted to New Historicism: "There are, at the site of New Historicism, at least two fields under cultivation; one is the Renaissance, the other, Romanticism."[3]

In the early 1990s, critics of the visionary poet William Blake began to see his work not as an isolated piece of individualism but as deeply embedded in the radical politics of the late 1790s. These ideas were solidified in a conference in 1990 entitled "Historicising Blake" and an edited collection which arose from it.[4] The seminal historicized study of Blake from the noted Marxist historian E.P. Thompson was published in 1993. Thompson sought to identify "Blake's tradition, [and] his particular situation within it," noting that to do so "involves some historical recovery, and attention to sources external to Blake."[5] Thompson's study can be read as New Historicist, although he did not label it as such. It is concerned with Blake's relationship with radical London and, consequently, his antithetical relationship with established power structures such as the church and state; Greenblatt's chapter in *Renaissance Self-Fashioning* on the dissidence of Christopher Marlowe works in a similar fashion.

Limitations

Renaissance Self-Fashioning's arguments that selves are fashioned in response to powerful social forces need not be read as uniquely culturally or geographically specific. However, Greenblatt constructs his arguments through a series of case studies of male, English authors of the late sixteenth and early seventeenth centuries. This focus does reveal a set of cultural assumptions on Greenblatt's part. Most obviously, it deals only with major figures of English literature (the courtier-poet Edmund Spenser, and prominent dramatists Christopher Marlowe and William Shakespeare) neglecting the range of writings from less culturally powerful writers; no women are discussed and no one from a cultural background that is not that of the English middle class. Only in the final chapter, on Shakespeare's play *Othello* (c.1603), do we see a model for female self-fashioning, the "erotic submission" of Desdemona.[6] This neglects the other voices and identities available to women in Renaissance England, as demonstrated by later critics, who have drawn on Greenblatt's methodology while rejecting his focus on male authors and figures.[7] Greenblatt examines America, the near East,* and Africa, but always as an English response to a foreign culture, not the culture itself.

This kind of cultural conditioning is, perhaps, a necessary consequence of any writing, and Greenblatt does acknowledge that his own position and background played a significant part in making the selections of texts and authors to link in *Renaissance Self-Fashioning*, noting that "literary criticism ... must be conscious of its own status as interpretation."[8] However, he does not reflect on the impact of these choices, or the ways in which they rely on a Western understanding of the development of world history through the colonial enterprise.

NOTES

1   Stephen Greenblatt, *Renaissance Self-Fashioning* 2nd ed. (Chicago: University of Chicago Press, 2005), xi.

2   Greenblatt, *Renaissance Self-Fashioning*, 1.

3   John H. Zammito, "Are We Being Theoretical Yet? The New Historicism, the New Philosophy of History, and "Practicing Historians"," *The Journal of Modern History* 65, no. 4 (1993) 789.

4   Steve Clark and David Worrall, eds., *Historicising Blake* (New York: St. Martin's Press, 1994).

5   E. P. Thompson, *Witness Against the Beast* (Cambridge: Cambridge University Press; 1994), xxiii.

6   Greenblatt, *Renaissance Self-Fashioning*, 244.

7   Linda Woodbridge, *Women and the English Renaissance: Literature and the Nature of Womankind, 1540 to 1620* (Champaign, IL: University of Illinois Press, 1984); Dympna Callaghan, *Women and Gender in Renaissance Tragedy* (Harlow: Harvester Wheatsheaf, 1989); Clare McManus, *Women on the Renaissance Stage: Anna of Denmark and Female Masquing in the Stuart Court (1590-1619)* (Manchester: Manchester University Press, 2002).

8   Greenblatt, *Renaissance Self-Fashioning*, 4.

PLACE IN THE AUTHOR'S WORK

KEY POINTS

- *Renaissance Self-Fashioning* was an early work, but the one which definitively established Greenblatt's reputation.

- Greenblatt has continued to follow the practices laid down in *Renaissance Self-Fashioning*, though he has gradually widened the scope of his enquiries.

- The work established New Historicism as a school of thought, and is still seen as a seminal text within that field.

Positioning

Renaissance Self-Fashioning was Stephen Greenblatt's second book, and the work that brought him major critical attention. His first book focused on the poet and explorer Sir Walter Raleigh, suggesting that his life should be viewed as a series of deliberate performances, designed to create a public persona to enhance his reputation and status. The original intent for *Renaissance Self-Fashioning* was to extend that project, showing that Raleigh was not unique in this ability, but was simply a particularly skilled example of a wider early modern social phenomenon. Instead, in the process of writing Greenblatt developed that concept into a general thesis concerning the formation of identity in the Renaissance, arguing that all identity is a construction in response to social or cultural pressure. The reverse, he suggested, is also true – the markers of identity we find in literary texts can reveal the power structures or social pressures to which they are a response. Greenblatt would later suggest that New Historicism, the critical school founded in and by *Renaissance Self-Fashioning*, is based upon "the proposition that a culture is a text."[1] Although he prefers the term

> **❝** *Renaissance Self-Fashioning* was the book in which I
> first found my own voice. **❞**
> Stephen Greenblatt, *Renaissance Self-Fashioning*

"poetics of culture" in *Renaissance Self-Fashioning*, the insistence upon
the interrelated nature of the literary text, historical context and
authorial biography clearly laid the pattern for the rest of Greenblatt's
long career as a literary critic.

Integration

During that career Greenblatt's interests, and critical style, have
remained consistent with those set out in *Renaissance Self-Fashioning*.
He continued the interest in the New World (primarily North
America) begun in Chapter Four on Spenser's epic *The Faerie Queene*
in a number of essays during the 1980s, culminating in a book–length
study, *Marvelous Possessions* in 1991. Throughout all of these works,
Greenblatt sees the New World as "a screen onto which the Europeans
projected their darkest and yet most compelling fantasies,"[2] and
therefore as a way of understanding what European writers perceived
as the pressures on their own society and lives. From the 1990s onward
his interests have largely turned to Shakespeare, in a manner similar to
the exploration of *Othello* carried out in chapter 6 of *Renaissance Self-
Fashioning*. He has written a number of articles on a variety of
Shakespeare's plays, as well as a full-length study of *Hamlet* (*Hamlet in
Purgatory* [2001]), focusing on the way in which changes in the belief
systems of Renaissance England, particularly of ghosts, influenced the
play. He has also produced a New Historicist biography of
Shakespeare, *Will in the World*, which draws links between
Shakespeare's biography, cultural context, and the recurring themes
of his drama.[3] In 2011, he released *The Swerve: How the Renaissance
Began*, which focuses on a single text, Lucretius's* *De Rerum Natura*

[*On the Nature of Things*]. This text, which had been thought lost, was rediscovered in the medieval period, and Greenblatt traces its influence, through copies, responses, and suppression, to "a great culture-wide explosion of interest in pagan antiquity" (that is, the Renaissance itself).[4] This argument is a classic piece of New Historicist criticism, using a single anecdote or text to demonstrate the "ripple effect" it had on culture, and the enormous shifts in society that are inscribed within literary texts.

Significance

Greenblatt's work has been among the most influential Renaissance criticism of the past 30 years. *Renaissance Self-Fashioning* substantially changed the landscape of early modern literary studies, and its methodology was highly influential within the school of thought known as (The) New Historicism. Greenblatt's subsequent work has only confirmed New Historicism as an important mode of criticism in the period. Scholars have criticized New Historicism for excluding marginalized voices, and it has now fallen somewhat out of fashion – at least in the purest sense of New Historicism as articulated by Greenblatt – but it is nonetheless a classic and important work in the development of English Literature as a field of study.

In some ways, the methodology of *Renaissance Self-Fashioning* depends on the work of Marxist critics, as well as social historians and anthropologists; however, it is the combination of ideas in *Renaissance Self-Fashioning* that is original: Greenblatt finds a way to put these social critiques together and apply them to a period that none of those thinkers was interested in. The importance of Greenblatt's work is that he opens up Renaissance literature to this kind of methodology. In doing so, he also shows that identities were formed, and social pressures enacted and resisted, much earlier than previous theorists like Foucault had ever claimed.

NOTES

1   Catherine Gallagher and Stephen Greenblatt, *Practicing New Historicism* (Chicago; London: University of Chicago Press, 2000), 14.

2   Stephen Greenblatt, *Renaissance Self-Fashioning* 2nd ed. (Chicago: University of Chicago Press, 2005), 181.

3   Stephen Greenblatt, *Will in the World: How Shakespeare Became Shakespeare* (London: Random House, 2004).

4   Stephen Greenblatt, *The Swerve: How the Renaissance Began* (London: Vintage, 2011), 13.

SECTION 3
IMPACT

THE FIRST RESPONSES

KEY POINTS

- *Renaissance Self-Fashioning* redefined the field of early modern literary studies, quickly becoming a dominant methodology.

- However, some groups noted that Greenblatt's study sidelined already marginalized groups still further.

- Later critics showed it was possible to use Greenblatt's methodology without necessarily accepting his view on how power structures society.

Criticism

The early responses to *Renaissance Self-Fashioning* were overwhelmingly positive. Prominent critics such as Louis Montrose* labeled the book "a seminal contribution to our necessary reinvention of the English Renaissance."[1] *Renaissance Self-Fashioning* was seen as offering a new methodology with which to approach sixteenth and seventeenth century material. Greenblatt's combination of social and psychological theory with historical detail offered a new model of an ideologically oriented mode of criticism that was eagerly accepted and built on by Renaissance scholars. This methodology quickly became highly influential in Renaissance studies, which moved from studying a narrow set of canonical writers to an appreciation of what non-canonical (or even apparently non-literary) texts revealed about the context from which they emerged.

However, this positive reception of the book's aims did not preclude critics from noticing certain structural issues. Jean Howard,* despite generally approving of the work, noted that the book's focus

> 66 The New Historicism erodes the firm ground of both criticism and literature. It tends to ask questions about its own methodological assumptions and those of others. 99
>
> Stephen Greenblatt, Introduction to *The Power of Forms in Renaissance Literature*

on individuals undermines its general aim of a wider commentary on broader cultural norms. She argued that by focusing on those six particular examples, Greenblatt suggests to the reader that they "transcended pervasive cultural paradigms for fashioning identity and left their marks *as individuals*."[2] Other critics noted that Greenblatt focused entirely on male self-fashioning, providing "a male protagonist whose centrality is never questioned,"[3] and neglecting female writers as well as the range of responses that Renaissance women produced from Renaissance men.

Most frequently, however, critics of *Renaissance Self-Fashioning* saw it as pessimistic in its treatment of individual agency. Greenblatt, they claimed, argues that powerful ideologies will always contain threats against them, and that individual choice is an illusion that masks the authoritarian forces determining human action. Jonathan Dollimore,* prominent amongst this movement, has noted that Greenblatt focuses too much on "the formative power of social and ideological structures which are both prior to experience and in some sense determining of it," rather than on the power of "human agency."[4]

Responses

Some critics did note that the insistence on focusing on a handful of prominent male figures undermined the validity of the broad claims that Greenblatt was making in the text. These critics, broadly of the feminist* school, have subsequently argued that *Renaissance Self-*

Fashioning (and New Historicism, the movement that developed around Greenblatt's methodology) ignores female voices and agency in favor of male-dominated power structures.[5] Greenblatt has never formally responded to such criticism, and his subsequent work has not altered in its focus on male writers from whom he can draw a generalized picture of Renaissance culture and practices.

Ten years after the publication of *Renaissance Self-Fashioning* in 1980, a noted critic of American literature commented that "New Historicists and feminists seem to talk at cross purposes, keeping their mutual distance, relegating each other to a kind of non-presence."[6] There has been no consensus or significant change in attitude in the years since. However, a parallel school of thought, known as Cultural Materialism,* has been developed to correct this perceived flaw in Greenblatt's methodology by concentrating on the success of radical or marginalized voices within a culture.

Greenblatt explicitly responds to this criticism in his preface to the 2005 edition of *Renaissance Self-Fashioning*. He accepts that on one level the book describes "an immense malevolent force determined to crush all resistance;"[7] however, he rejects the idea that this should be the dominant reading of the text, suggesting instead that his work chronicles "hope in many different forms, often crushed but then springing up in spite of everything."[8] Greenblatt's response, then, is not to change his critical practice, but to challenge the interpretation of that practice. This has not proved sufficiently persuasive to convince all the critics of his work that it is in fact a "hopeful" text, and debate continues about the extent to which an individual can escape from his or her culture, and whether Renaissance texts show a totalizing power, or the possibility of subverting or destabilizing power.

Conflict and Consensus

In 1982, Greenblatt argued in his introduction to *The Power of Forms* that a consensus had formed around his position, noting that "recent criticism has been less concerned to establish the organic unity of literary works," instead focusing on "the jostling of orthodox and subversive influences."[9] However, this apparent consensus has nonetheless subtly drifted away from Greenblatt's original focus over time, borrowing large parts of his historicist methods, but not applying it to the same, political end.

By the middle of the 1980s, other critics such as Jonathan Goldberg were developing New Historicism. Goldberg's work continues to see the text and author as determined by culture, but prioritizes the theoretical and psychoanalytical elements of *Renaissance Self-Fashioning*, using thinkers such as Derrida* to examine both the text and its context.[10] Similarly, the school of thought known as queer theory,* which rejects the idea of an "essential" or "universal human" and instead looks at the constructed nature of identity, has moved away from "the new historicist tendency to cast the past in terms of difference."[11] This is not, though, a complete rejection of New Historicism; rather, some queer theorists, such as Jeremy Webster, use historicist methods as a jumping-off point to understand and chart the development of sexualities, even as they stress the discontinuities between the sixteenth century and the present day.[12]

NOTES

1   Louis Adrian Montrose, "A Poetics of Renaissance Culture: Review of *Renaissance Self-Fashioning*," *Criticism* 23, no. 4 (1981): 359.

2   Jean E. Howard, "The Cultural Construction Of the Self in The Renaissance: Review of *Renaissance Self-Fashioning*," *Shakespeare Quarterly* 34, no. 3: 380.

3   Margaret Waller, "Academic Tootsie: The Denial of Difference and the Difference It Makes: Review of *Renaissance Self-Fashioning*," *Diacritics* 17, no. 1: 3.

4   Jonathan Dollimore, "Introduction: Shakespeare, cultural materialism and the new historicism," in *Political Shakespeare*, ed. Jonathan Dollimore and Alan Sinfield (Manchester: Manchester University Press), 3.

5   See Carol Thomas Neely, "Constructing the Subject: Feminist Practice and the New Renaissance Discourses," *English Literary Renaissance* 18, no. 1 (Winter 1988): 5-18. For a feminist use of New Historicism, see M. Bella Mirabella, "Feminist Self-Fashioning: Christine de Pizan and The Treasure of the City of Ladies," *European Journal of Women's Studies* 6 (1999): 9-20.

6   Wai-Chee Dimock, "Feminism, New Historicism, and the Reader," *American Literature* 63: 601.

7   Stephen Greenblatt, *Renaissance Self-Fashioning* 2nd ed. (Chicago: University of Chicago Press, 2005), xvi.

8   Greenblatt, *Renaissance Self-Fashioning*, xvi.

9   Stephen Greenblatt, ed., *The Power of Forms in the English Renaissance* (Norman, OK: Pilgrim Books, 1982), 5-6.

10 Jonathan Goldberg, *Voice Terminal Echo* (New York: Methuen, 1986).

11 Paula Blank, "The Proverbial 'Lesbian': Queering Etymology in Contemporary Critical Practice," *Modern Philology* 109, no. 1 (2011): 123.

12 J. W. Webster, "Queering the Seventeenth Century: Historicism, Queer Theory, and Early Modern Literature," *Literature Compass*, 5 (2008): 376–393.

MODULE 10
THE EVOLVING DEBATE

KEY POINTS

- Greenblatt remains an important figure within early modern, specifically New Historicist, literary criticism

- Though now nuanced from its original statement on *Renaissance Self-Fashioning*, New Historicism remains an influential school of thought.

- Scholars still focus on authority and resistance, and the methodology has become attractive to post-colonial* theorists.

Uses and Problems

Stephen Greenblatt himself continues to be an influential proponent of New Historicism. His 2004 biography of Shakespeare, *Will in the World*, was in effect a New Historicist biography; beginning with the words "Let us imagine," the text skips past the traditional details and scholarship of a biography (property, schooling, investments, intellectual circles), focusing instead on the potential details of Shakespeare's life that can be inferred from the traces in his plays.[1] The "imagining" that opens the book is of a nursery rhyme that Greenblatt claims Shakespeare likely heard as a child because it recurs in his play *King Lear* (c.1605–6).

However, other scholarship has accepted his historicist ideas without necessarily applying the methodology of subjection and resistance that animates *Renaissance Self-Fashioning*. The critics following this kind of approach are not as interested as Greenblatt in power structures, and many would question whether the individual is as powerless in the face of powerful ideologies or belief structures as

> **❝** This book ... aims to discover the actual person who wrote the most important body of imaginative literature of the last thousand years. Or rather, since the actual person is a matter of well-documented public record, it aims to tread the shadowy paths that lead from the life he lived into the literature he created. **❞**
>
> Stephen Greenblatt, *Will in the World*

Greenblatt suggests. The prominent cultural scholar Andrew Hadfield* has identified a move among critics to "consider the resistance to the explicable and the easily summarized in literature, in order to suggest what makes works of art distinctive."[2] That is, they reject Greenblatt's idea that there is a broad "poetics of culture", a general sense of power relations and structures, and identifying this can "explain" a work of art. The debate around Greenblatt's work, then, is not whether or not his historicizing methodology is worthwhile, but what the application of that method tells us about power structures and the possibility of radical resistance to them.

Recent work on Shakespeare, for example, puts his work in the context of the educational systems of the Renaissance, or the Bible, or Renaissance ideas of fatherhood.[3] Though critics may disagree on which of these contexts is the most important, they all agree that Shakespeare's work needs to be seen not as something standing apart from its time, but powerfully influenced by it. These critical approaches to Shakespeare are also linked by the broad trend in historicist studies of moving away from Greenblatt's generalized, long-view study towards very specific, local contexts for individual texts.

Schools of Thought

The methodology Greenblatt sets out in the book – reading canonical texts alongside lesser-known works and historical documentation in order to develop a better sense of the context that influences the development of literature – has now become the standard model for approaching and discussing Renaissance literature with a school of thought developing under the name "New Historicism" – though Greenblatt initially resisted that term (preferring his own formulation "poetics of culture"[4]), since he felt that the label "New Historicism" placed too much emphasis on traditional "history," rather than the social anthropology (or study of culture) that he felt was the driving force behind *Renaissance Self-Fashioning*.

New Historicism took root mainly in America, where Greenblatt was writing (he was a professor at the University of California, Berkeley, when *Renaissance Self-Fashioning* was published). Major critics such as Jean Howard adopted the New Historicist methodology in their own work.[5] Louis Montrose is perhaps the most prominent among the followers of Greenblatt. He has continued to work on questions of ideology and power, and his recent book on Elizabeth I (reigned 1588-1603) continues New Historicist methodology by focusing on the "powers ascribed to the Elizabethan royal image and powers addressed against it."[6] Critics of major authors, especially those considered by Greenblatt in *Renaissance Self-Fashioning*, also began to adopt New Historicism. Scholars working on the courtier poet Edmund Spenser's epic *The Faerie Queene* (1596) had traditionally been interested in the allegories and structure of the poem;[7] however, following Greenblatt's work, which showed that the poem was "yoked to the service of a reality forever outside of itself" (Queen Elizabeth),[8] critics have focused on the culture in which Spenser was working, and especially the issues of gender he had to confront in writing for a female monarch.[9] New Historicism remained influential throughout the 1990s, and leading critics and editors such as Stephen Orgel (a contemporary of Greenblatt) continue to follow the New Historicist model.

In Current Scholarship

Greenblatt's interest in power and performance was in some ways preempted by the work of Stephen Orgel. Writing in 1975, Orgel noted the way in which royal and theatrical power intertwined, especially in the court masque,* which he argued "presents the triumph of an aristocratic community; at its center is a belief in the hierarchy and a faith in the power of idealization."[10] *Renaissance Self-Fashioning* complicated that relationship, showing that art did more than simply reflect prevailing discourse, and Orgel's later work has been influenced by this methodology, seeing the stage as a site of cultural and political contest, rather than reflecting a single ideology.[11]

Leonard Tennenhouse is another (relatively) direct disciple of Greenblatt's work. Like Greenblatt, his primary focus is on William Shakespeare, arguing that "Shakespeare uses his drama to authorize political authority, and political authority as he represents it, in turn authorizes art."[12] This is a clear development from the principles of *Renaissance Self-Fashioning*, which argues that "Shakespeare relentlessly *explores* the relations of power."[13] Tennenhouse follows Greenblatt in seeing that "during the Renaissance, political imperatives were also aesthetic imperatives."[14] For both Greenblatt and Tennenhouse, Shakespearean drama derives its force as a work of art by offering a legitimization of the established political system, especially the monarchy.

Athough Greenblatt's historicist methodology has become largely commonplace (an influence of New Historicism as well as parallel movements such as Cultural Materialism), the political aspects of New Historicism remain the subject of debate. H. Aram Veeser argued in the introduction to the influential collection of essays, *The New Historicism*, first published in 1989 and reissued in 2013, that "crisis not consensus surrounds the New Historicists project" since it has been "kept off-balance by internal stresses."[15] One important essay in that collection, by Gayatri Spivak,* argued that New Historicism was more or less incompatible with post-colonial criticism; in her view,

New Historicist ideas of "history," when applied to the "nationhood" and "citizenship" of the post-colonial space, privileges colonial history, not the "subaltern"* who has their history written over.[16]

NOTES

1   Stephen Greenblatt, *Will in the World: How Shakespeare Became Shakespeare* (London: Random House, 2004), 23.

2   Andrew Hadfield, "The Relevance of Spenser," *Modern Philology* 106, no. 4 (2009): 687.

3   Lynn Enterline, *Shakespeare's Schoolroom: Rhetoric, Discipline, Emotion* (Philadelphia: University of Pennsylvania Press, 2012); Travis DeCook and Alan Galey, eds., *Shakespeare, the Bible, and the Form of the Book: Contested Scriptures* (London: Routledge, 2012); Tom McFaul, *Problem Fathers in Shakespeare and Renaissance Drama* (Cambridge: Cambridge University Press, 2012).

4   Stephen Greenblatt, *Renaissance Self-Fashioning* 2nd ed. (Chicago: University of Chicago Press, 2005), 5.

5   Jean E. Howard, *The Stage and Social Struggle in Early Modern England* (London: Routledge, 1994).

6   Louis Adrian Montrose, *The Subject of Elizabeth: Authority, Gender, and Representation* (Chicago: University of Chicago Press, 2006), 5.

7   Alastair Fowler, *Spenser and the Numbers of Time* (London: Routledge, 1964).

8   Greenblatt, *Renaissance Self-Fashioning*, 192;

9   See Maureen Quilligan, "The Comedy of Female Authority in *The Faerie Queene*," *English Literary Renaissance* 17(1987).

10 Stephen Orgel, *The Illusion of Power: Political Theater in the English Renaissance* (Berkeley and Los Angeles, CA: University of California Press, 1975), 40.

11 Stephen Orgel, *Impersonations: The Performance of Gender in Shakespeare's England* (Cambridge: Cambridge University Press, 1996).

12 Leonard Tennenhouse, "Strategies of State and Political Plays: *A Midsummer Night's Dream, Henry IV, Henry V, Henry VIII*," in *Political Shakespeare*, ed. Jonathan Dollimore and Alan Sinfield (Manchester: Manchester University Press), 111.

13 Greenblatt, *Renaissance Self-Fashioning*, 254.

14 Tennenhouse, "Strategies of State and Political Plays", 125.

15 H. Aram Veeser, "Introduction" in *The New Historicism*, ed. H. Aram Veeser (London: Routledge, 2013), xv.

16 Gayatri Chakravorty Spivak, "The New Historicism: Political Commitment and the Post-modern critic" in *The New Historicism*, ed. Veeser, 282.

IMPACT AND INFLUENCE TODAY

KEY POINTS

- *Renaissance Self-Fashioning* is the classic articulation of an important theoretical position.

- The use of the anecdote as a historical method has been an important methodological battleground.

- Recent scholarship has sought to balance the historical work of Greenblatt and his followers with a renewed attention to the internal tensions of the text.

Position

Renaissance Self-Fashioning remains one of the core texts within the field of study of Renaissance literature. The ideas and methodologies it sets out became the founding principles of the intellectual movement known as New Historicism, which aims to interrogate texts alongside their context in order to discern the power relations that existed within society at the time of writing. The basic methodology that Greenblatt suggests has been widely adopted. Most critical engagements with early modern literature now follow – at least to some extent – Greenblatt's methods of placing the literary text alongside other cultural and historical documents, even if they do not necessarily share Greenblatt's concern with the structures of power, or psychology of individual authors, in the Renaissance. Renaissance scholars therefore frequently return to *Renaissance Self-Fashioning*, or texts that have built on or developed its ideas, to ground their methodological practices.

Though the historicizing methodology put forward by *Renaissance Self-Fashioning* (and other contemporary texts) has been largely

> **❝** Explication and paraphrase are not enough; we seek something more, something that the authors we study would not have had sufficient distance upon themselves and their own era to grasp. **❞**
>
> Catherine Gallagher and Stephen Greenblatt, *Practicing New Historicism*

accepted, the conclusions Greenblatt draws have been more keenly debated. For example, questions have been raised over how far the pervasive power structures that Greenblatt identifies would have been felt by those contemporary to the texts he analyzes: "only those plays that were blatantly obvious in their agendas could have accomplished much New Historicist-style work."[1] Whether one believes that all, some, or no pieces of early modern culture would have "accomplished" the "work" of critiquing or representing power, the fact that this question is being asked in the terms of New Historicism is a recognition of the impact of that theoretical position.

Interaction

One of the most pervasive criticisms of Greenblatt's work in general, and *Renaissance Self-Fashioning* in particular, is that he is over-reliant on the anecdote; that is, the incidents which he discusses are individual moments, not part of a larger pattern, and so the social insight that can be gleaned from them is minimal. The anecdote "functions not as evidence … but as trope".[2] Consequently, for these critics Greenblatt's use of history must be partial; the things he claims are connected are in fact a series of more or less random events that he has yoked together by imposing his own narrative, which assumes the connections it is attempting to prove.

New Historicists such as Catherine Gallagher* have offered a spirited defense of the anecdote. In *Practicing New Historicism*, a volume of essays she co-edited with Stephen Greenblatt, Gallagher argued that "often an anecdote incompletely digested by the larger narrative divulges a different reality, which is behind or beside the narrative surface."[3] Gallagher revealed some skepticism towards the anecdote, not least when it is pulled into the kind of totalizing history which New Historicism resists. However, in her essays within *Practicing New Historicism* she argues, and then shows, that properly used it is a valuable part of understanding the past, revealing thoughts and currents of resistance that would otherwise be unavailable to the literary historian.

The Continuing Debate

Although New Criticism has now been largely supplanted by New Historicism, there are still critics, such as Harold Bloom, who see literature as a phenomenon entirely separate from culture and politics. He argues instead that great poets react only to their predecessors in a "battle between strong equals;"[4] literature thus becomes a sequence of poetic struggles and inversions, with a regard only for poetic tradition, not contemporary events or ideas. Though Bloom's influence has waned within Renaissance criticism, he maintains considerable authority across academia as a whole, and has continued to attack what he terms as "the New Cynicism" (a cluster of critical tendencies that are rooted in French theories of culture and encompass the New Historicism and its ilk).[5]

   Renaissance Self-Fashioning also offers a challenge to the critics of the authors that Greenblatt focuses on in the text. Although Shakespeare criticism has now turned towards a historicist methodology reminiscent of Greenblatt and his contemporaries (even if their local concerns differ from power and resistance that are the hallmarks of *Renaissance Self-Fashioning*), critics of the courtier poet Edmund Spenser (1552-99) have been more divided. Spenser's allegorical epic poem *The Faerie Queene* (1596) is discussed by Greenblatt as a glorification of state power "yoked to the service of a reality forever outside of itself,"[6] the court of Queen Elizabeth. However, the allegorical nature of the poem has invited a number of readings of *The Faerie Queene* as a self-contained text, focused on explaining the poem by decoding the allegorical figures and ideas it presents and repeats throughout.[7] Though this remains a prominent method of reading Spenser, it has been challenged by New Historicists, chiefly Louis Montrose, who has followed Greenblatt's recognition of the importance of Elizabeth to *The Faerie Queene*.[8] More recently, there has been a turn back towards the literary qualities of the poem, as scholars "reject literature as ideologically loaded" in response to a single power structure, and focus instead on the "complexity and balance" within the poem.[9] In this way, *Renaissance Self-Fashioning*, and its disciples, continues to contribute to debates within Renaissance criticism.

NOTES

1   Robert D. Hume, "The Socio-Politics of London Comedy from Jonson to Steele," *Huntington Library Quarterly* 74, no. 2 (2011): 216.

2   David Scott Kastan, "Shakespeare After Theory," in *Opening the Borders: Inclusivity in Early Modern Studies* ed. James V. Mirollo and Peter C. Herman (Newark, DE: University of Delaware Press, 2003), 206-225 (212).

3   Catherine Gallagher, "Counterhistory and the Anecdote," in *Practicing New Historicism,* ed. Catherine Gallagher and Stephen Greenblatt (Chicago: Chicago University Press, 2000), 49-74 (51).

4   Harold Bloom, *The Anxiety of Influence: A Theory of Poetry*, 2nd ed. (Oxford: Oxford University Press, 1997), 11.

5   Harold Bloom, *The Anatomy of Influence* (New Haven, CT: Yale University Press, 2011), 8.

6   Stephen Greenblatt, *Renaissance Self-Fashioning* 2nd ed. (Chicago: University of Chicago Press, 2005), 192.

7   Alastair Fowler, *Spenser and the Numbers of Time* (London: Routledge, 1964); Harry Berger, Jr, *Revisionary Play: Studies in the Spenserian Dynamics* (Berkeley, CA: University of California Press, 1988).

8   Louis Adrian Montrose, "The Elizabethan Subject and the Spenserian Text," in *Literary Theory / Renaissance Texts*, ed. Patricia Parker and David Quint (Baltimore: Johns Hopkins University Press, 1986).

9   Andrew Hadfield, "The Relevance of Spenser," *Modern Philology* 106, no. 4 (2009): 688.

MODULE 12
WHERE NEXT?

KEY POINTS

- *Renaissance Self-Fashioning* now largely supports current debates and methodologies, rather than being a topic of debate itself.

- Some scholars still use the text to investigate specific problems, but few wholeheartedly identify with New Historicism as a school of thought.

- *Renaissance Self-Fashioning* is still hugely important because of how embedded its practices and methodologies are within the discipline.

Potential

Renaissance Self-Fashioning continues to generate wide-ranging debate across academic disciplines, as new generations of scholars read and react to it. Though its polemic style, (supposed) pessimism and cultural biases are acknowledged, it is also still regarded as an important intervention into fundamental issues such as power and selfhood. Greenblatt's text continues to influence much contemporary work done in the field of Renaissance literature and beyond, and seems likely to do so for the foreseeable future. However, it is likely to do that indirectly – though scholarship in an explicitly New Historicist fashion does still exist, it tends to be focused on the internal mechanics of a particular text or author, rather than the broad "poetics of culture" that Greenblatt aimed at.

The most widespread version of this influence is the range of sources that are now considered alongside canonical literary texts: reading Shakespeare alongside contemporary ballads, Marlowe with

> **❝**[W]hile scholarship dealing explicitly with New Historicist, deconstructive, and psychoanalytic methodologies [among others] are rarer today than they were decades ago, the central lessons of these theoretical approaches persist, even if only tacitly, in much of our field's best work.**❞**
>
> Jess Keiser, "The Passion for the New."

religious sceptics and occultists, or Milton* with political or economic theorists is now so commonplace as to be unremarkable. In some ways, the ubiquity of the methodology of New Historicism has eroded the influence of *Renaissance Self-Fashioning*: the ideas it puts forward, which were radical and game-changing in 1980, are now familiar. What has remained important is the practice of reading "literature and culture with an eye for those elements that, seen from the perspective of dominant critical opinion, appear as odd, contradictory, or even destabilizing to our current ways of reading and knowing."[1]

Future Directions

Few young scholars today would explicitly describe themselves as New Historicist. The newer generation of academic researchers tends to focus on the historicizing elements of Greenblatt's work, without the emphasis on power, looking instead to place the literary text within other contexts such as gender or culture. All but the most avowedly theoretical project on early modern English literature will include writing and politics contemporary to the author under discussion, and while *Renaissance Self-Fashioning* helped to set that direction in the field, this kind of historicism is now so well established as a methodology (and draws on a number of critical schools beyond New Historicism) that there is no need to return to *Renaissance Self-Fashioning* to justify it.

Nevertheless, some scholars have developed applications of Greenblatt's work in new fields of enquiry. Richard Burt, a professor in English and Film at the University of Florida has recently returned to Greenblatt's work in his study of the way in which Medieval and Renaissance technology is depicted in film. Here, he focuses on "New Historicism's interest in spectrality" to think about the "reanimation, repetitions, and doublings" inherent in film that shows the manual copying of monks or the early printing press.[2] This kind of work seems the most likely future direction for *Renaissance Self-Fashioning* (and Greenblatt's corpus more generally), picking up on broad, interdisciplinary themes as part of projects in innovative sub-fields such as adaptations of literature or digital humanities.*

Summary

Renaissance Self-Fashioning fundamentally changed the way in which critics approach early modern literature. Shifting the focus from the text as a self-contained work of art, Greenblatt argued that literature needed to be seen within the context of the society that produced it. He argued that it was possible to perceive the workings of powerful social forces, such as church, state, and family, in the interactions between the text and its culture. He analyzes literature using his own mix of ideas from cultural anthropology, history, and literary studies, to reveal the power structures, ideologies, and anxieties that condition the text. *Renaissance Self-Fashioning* was the first coherent articulation of this methodology, and is the foundational document of the school of thought that became known as New Historicism.

Greenblatt has continued to develop the ideas presented in *Renaissance Self-Fashioning* throughout his career, particularly focusing on the Renaissance itself, William Shakespeare, and the sense of wonder evoked by the discovery and colonization of the New World (the Americas). He remains an important and influential critic.

New Historicism is now deeply embedded within early modern critical practice; Scholars rarely now choose to discuss Renaissance texts without considering the social, political, and cultural contexts from which they emerge. Scholars continue to expand Greenblatt's practice, finding new contexts to consider, and expanding the range of authors examined. New Historicism therefore looks set to continue as a key methodology for understanding early modern literature, although the school of thought associated with the term (that is by no means a singular methodology) continues to evolve and develop in ways that have moved far beyond Greenblatt's text.

However, Greenblatt's work in close reading the authors and texts he selects is still as engaging and thought-provoking as it was when it was first published. The work contained in *Renaissance Self-Fashioning* is rich and varied, and the range and depth of Greenblatt's scholarship remains a powerful driving force for Renaissance criticism. Returning to this foundational text can be a rewarding experience for students and scholars alike, and *Renaissance Self-Fashioning* continues to be the most compelling argument for the New Historicist methodology it sets forth.

NOTES

1   Jess Keiser, "The Passion for the New." *Eighteenth-Century Studies*, vol. 50 no. 3, 2017, 337-340 (337).

2   Richard Burt, *Medieval and Early Modern Film and Media* (New York: Palgrave, 2016), 3.

GLOSSARY

GLOSSARY OF TERMS

Anglocentricism: A study or world view that puts the English-speaking world (normally the UK and USA) at its center, to the exclusion or detriment of other viewpoints.

Authoritarianism: A form of political organization marked by a strong government (often headed by a single, powerful leader). Individuals in this system often have limited freedom, since they are expected to follow laws and orders, often on pain of harsh punishment.

Courtier: Someone who served an aristocrat or monarch in person, often living inside (or near) a residence or royal palace. These included close advisers (both domestic and military), entertainers, writers, clergy, and administrators. Being "at court" was regarded as a great honor, and opportunity for advancement.

Cultural Anthropology: The study of the cultures of distinct human groups (such as nationalities, tribes, or societies), often in a comparative way with other groups. "Culture" does not necessarily refer to cultural production (art, literature, and so on), but a way of experiencing the world, and explaining that worldview to others.

Cultural Materialism: The English school of Cultural Materialism borrows many of Greenblatt's methods and influences, but focuses not on centralized power structures but on marginalized voices.

Dialecticism: A model of thought or debate in which two opposite positions are held against each other, with the ultimate goal of finding an objective truth through discussion and comparison.

Digital Humanities: The application of scientific or computational tools to the study of artistic works. In literature, this often takes the form of large-scale data projects such as searches in a number of digitized texts, or creating relational schemes for correspondence or narrative structure.

Early Modern: A period in history that marks the end of the medieval period and the beginnings of the modern world. Because of this, it is usually used to refer to concepts or innovations rather than time, but can be loosely dated 1500-1800.

Epic: A long narrative poem, usually set in the distant past, dealing with the heroic deeds of a great figure in the history of a nation, who overcomes both natural and supernatural trials.

Feminism: As an umbrella term for a number of different approaches, "feminism" can be understood as the theory and practice of seeking equality between men and women, and addressing the structural biases that prevent such equality. This might be a theoretical untangling of sex and gender, or very practical action on women's rights or equal pay.

Humanism: A collection of philosophical and moral ideas, all of which emphasize the potential of the human to develop and play a part in his or her community. Humanism in the Renaissance focused on developing the disciplines we know now as the humanities (history, politics, literature) to enrich life and encourage virtue. Though the term is now often used to mean secular, or anti-religious, groups, in the Renaissance many influential religious thinkers were also humanists, seeking to reconcile classical learning with scriptural values.

Ideology: A system of thought and/or power that attempts to present itself as the "natural" way for things to be organized (capitalism and communism, for example).

Marxism: Founded by the German socio-economic thinker Karl Marx, Marxism investigates the conflict between social classes as a result of the exploitation of those who are forced to sell their labor (the *proletariat*) by those who own the means of production, or capital (the *bourgeoisie*). A Marxist is someone who adheres to these theories, or uses them as the basis of further intellectual inquiry.

Masque: A form of royal or aristocratic entertainment, popular in the seventeenth and eighteenth centuries. Masques combine music, dancing, and drama, and usually involve lavish sets, props, and costumes.

Medieval: A period in European history, stretching approximately from the fifth to the fifteenth century C.E. The period was one of initial decline after the collapse of the Roman Empire and then a recovery in population, trade, technology, culture, and exploration across a number of European states that were first formed in this period.

Nationalism: A political and cultural ideology that prioritizes the nation, and the idea of belonging to a nation, above all else, often in opposition to an international or global perspective.

Near East: A historical term for the countries which border the Eastern parts of the Mediterranean (such as Greece, Turkey, and Egypt), in contrast to the Far East of China, Japan and India. Now generally referred to as the Middle East.

New Criticism: A way of reading literature that excludes all context, focusing entirely on qualities of the work of art as it is presented.

New Historicism: A way of reading literature that focuses on the cultural and social conditions of its creation, either to explain the work of art itself or to discover something about that context.

Post-Colonialism: The study of the aftermaths and legacies of colonialism (the forcible settlement of territory and/or people by another nation), in particular the thought and culture of those former colonies that have become independent.

Postmodernism: A broad intellectual movement in arts, philosophy and architecture, dating to the latter part of the twentieth century. Postmodernists reject claims to universality, stressing that concepts such as "truth" or "beauty" can only ever be partial and subjective.

Pulitzer Prize: The Pulitzer foundation (est. 1917) awards 21 prizes per year for outstanding work in American journalism and the arts, including the best piece of journalism, novel, biography, play, and work of history.

Psychoanalysis: A way of understanding the unconscious mind and its relationship with the conscious mind. In particular, it deals with hidden conflicts or impulses and how they impact upon a patient's life (or, in art and literature, their cultural productions).

Queer Theory: An examination of behaviours such as homosexual desire and cross-dressing to show how sex, gender, and sexuality are not automatically aligned but are culturally conditioned.

Reformation: A series of religious upheavals across Europe (c.1517-1648) as a number of thinkers and preachers broke away from what they saw as the corrupt Catholic Church, founding Protestant churches (including, eventually, the Church of England).

Renaissance: A cultural shift that took place in Europe approximately 1300-1700, and flourished in England during the sixteenth and early seventeenth centuries. Sparked by the rediscovery of texts of classical Greece and Rome, scholars across Europe revived and reconsidered ancient ideas and their modern applications.

Romanticism: A movement that placed a high value on sensory experience, especially the production of emotion. The Romantics argued that poets and artists had a special sensibility, often in affinity with nature, which could be articulated and communicated through art and literature. Key poets in this movement are William Wordsworth (1770-1850), Percy Bysshe Shelley (1792-1822), and John Keats (1795-1821).

Subaltern: A term used by postcolonial scholars to denote those who are outside of the power structures of the colony and their colonial overlords. This exclusion may be for any reason, including race, class, gender, politics, or geography.

Vietnam War (1955-75): The conflict in Vietnam began as a civil war between the communist North Vietnamese and the capitalist South; the United States backed the South in order to prevent a communist takeover. The war was largely fought between US forces and the guerrilla forces of the North (Viet Cong), with significant casualties of both Vietnamese civilians and US soldiers.

PEOPLE MENTIONED IN THE TEXT

Louis Althusser (1918-1990) was a Marxist philosopher from French Algeria. He fought in the World War II, and was a longstanding member of the French Communist party. His work focused on the writings of Karl Marx, and in particular the ways in which the structures of power in society acted on the individual.

C. L. [Cesar Lombardi] Barber (1913-1980) was a noted critic of Renaissance drama, especially Shakespeare and Marlowe.

William Blake (1757-1827) was a radical poet and artist. His work combined images and text to create a visionary world of his own personal mythology, which challenged the traditional church and social structures of his time.

Harold Bloom (b. 1930) is an American critic, currently the Sterling Professor of Humanities at Yale University. He is most famous for his theory of influence that has been worked out through his career, in which poets and writers continually struggle against their literary forebears.

Cleanth Brooks (1906-1994) was a literary critic and theorist, who spent the major part of his career at Yale. He was a leading proponent of the New Criticism, a school of thought that saw the literary text as a complete, symbolic artefact to be studied in terms of its wholeness, and how it achieves that wholeness.

Jacques Derrida (1930-2000) was an Algerian-born French philosopher and literary critic. His work addresses the form and function of language, arguing that all language is inherently unstable, as it can be only defined through its relations to other language, not to any "real" phenomena.

John Donne (1572-1631) was a poet and clergyman. The first part of his career is characterized by erotic love poetry, and the second half, after he became a clergyman in 1615 then Dean of St Paul's Cathedral in 1621, by deep religious speculation on the nature of God.

Elizabeth I Tudor (1533-1603; reigned 1558-1603) was Queen of England and Ireland. Her reign is often called a "golden period," because she brought an end to religious fighting in England and ushered in a period of stability, which allowed the arts to flourish.

Catherine Gallagher (b. 1945) is the Eggers Professor of English Literature at Berkeley. She is a prominent New Historicist, as well as being a scholar of women writers.

Clifford Geertz (1926-2006) was an American anthropologist. He was interested in the way in which symbols and symbolic behaviour influenced society and cultural development.

Michel Foucault (1926-84) was a French philosopher and social critic, whose work is characterized by an interest in how prevailing cultural assumptions and social structures create identity.

Jonathan Goldberg (b. 1943) is a literary theorist and critic, currently Arts and Sciences Distinguished Professor Emeritus of English at Emory University. His work often blends psychoanalysis and literary criticism.

Andrew Hadfield is Professor of English at the University of Sussex. His research concerns the intersection between literature and politics in the early modern period, with a focus on Spenser and travel writing.

Christopher Hill (1912–2003) was a prominent historian and master of Balliol College, Oxford. His work focused on early modern politics and revolutionaries, especially those prominent during the English Civil War (1642–9).

Jean E. Howard (b. 1948) is the George Delacorte Professor in the Humanities at Columbia University, New York. A prominent New Historicist, she focuses on early modern drama and poetry from the theoretical perspectives of Marxism and feminism.

Lisa Jardine (1944–2015) was a Professor at University College London, a noted historian and public intellectual. Her work was wide-ranging, but usually concerned with the global history of the Renaissance (with subjects as diverse as literature, cartography, and art history), as well as feminist readings of Renaissance drama.

Jacques Lacan (1901–81) was a French psychiatrist and psychoanalyst. He argued that language, which is socially constructed, could never adequately express the inner experiences of the self, or the unconscious mind.

Lucretius (c. 99–55 B.C.E.) was a Roman poet. He is now best known for *De Rerum Natura [On the Nature of Things]*, an epic poem about the beginnings of the universe.

Christopher Marlowe (1564–93) was an English playwright, poet, and translator, noted in his own time as a writer of tragic drama. His literary career lasted just six (very productive) years before he was killed in a tavern brawl, leading some scholars to speculate that he was secretly a spy, a Catholic, or homosexual.

John Milton (1608-1674) was an English poet and propagandist. He is most famous for his epic poem *Paradise Lost* (1667), which tells of the fall of Adam and Eve, but he was also an active prose writer in support of republicanism.

Louis Adrian Montrose is a literary scholar, currently Rebeca Hickel Emeritus Professor of Elizabethan Studies at the University of San Diego. He is closely associated with New Historicism and works on Renaissance literature, particularly on representations of Queen Elizabeth I.

Karl Marx (1818-83) was born in Prussia (modern day Germany). His work on political economy focused on the way society functioned through classes, especially the distinctions between the laboring class and the bourgeoisie, the ruling class who controlled society through their ownership of the means of production (such as factories).

Jerome McGann (b. 1937) is an American literary critic, currently the John Stewart Bryan Professor at the University of Virginia. He primarily studies eighteenth and nineteenth century writers, attempting to combine detailed textual criticism with an awareness of contextual and political influences on the text.

Sir Thomas More (1478-1535) was the Lord Chancellor and advisor to King Henry VIII. He was a lawyer, statesman, and author, famous for his *Utopia*, an imaginary land of plenty and perfect social order.

Richard Nixon (1913-1994) was the 37th President of the United States (1969-1974). He ended American involvement in the war in Vietnam, but was forced to resign his office in disgrace over the Watergate scandal, a cover-up of a break in at his political opponent's headquarters in the Watergate Hotel.

Stephen Orgel (b. 1933) is the Jackson Eli Reynolds Professor of the Humanities at Stanford University. He has written widely on the political aspects of Renaissance culture.

Sir Walter Raleigh (1554–1618) was an English explorer, pirate, courtier, and writer. He was involved in early colonial enterprises in Virginia and Guyana, but was arrested and executed for piracy against Spanish treasure ships in 1618 (in order to ease relations between England and Spain).

William Shakespeare (1564–1616) was a noted actor, playwright, and poet. Now widely renowned as England's greatest ever dramatist, he was born in Stratford and moved to London, where he wrote a large number of plays under royal patronage, as well as a long sequence of sonnets.

Edmund Spenser (1552–99) was a noted poet and a colonial administrator in Ireland. He became famous for the pastoral (country) poem *The Shepheardes Calendar* (1579), and the allegorical epic *The Faerie Queene* (1596).

Gayatri Chakravorty Spivak (b. 1942) is a Professor at Columbia University, New York. She is a noted postcolonial critic and poststructuralist theorist.

E. P. Thomson (1924–1993) was an influential literary and historical critic. Working within a Marxist tradition, his work focused on the development of the working class in England, and the radicalism of working-class writers and thinkers.

William Tyndale (c. 1494–1536) was an English Protestant reformer. He is mostly known for his translation of the Bible into English in

1526. He was burned as a heretic for his translation, which was deemed to be against the teachings of the Catholic Church.

Raymond Williams (1921-88) was an influential Marxist critic and philosopher, whose work pioneered an approach to a cultural reading of texts by recovering the "structures of feeling" (that is, actual lived experience and response to power) of historical subjects.

Thomas Wyatt (c.1503-42) was an English poet and diplomat. He is credited with popularizing the sonnet form in English.

WORKS CITED

WORKS CITED

Althusser, Louis. "Ideology and Ideological State Apparatuses." In *The Anthropology of the State: A Reader*, ed. Aradhana Sharma and Akhil Gupta. Oxford: Blackwell, 2006.

Barber, C.L. *Shakespeare's Festive Comedy: A Study of Dramatic Form and its Relation to Social Custom*. Princeton, N.J.: Princeton University Press, 1959. Reissued with a foreword by Stephen Greenblatt 2012.

Bella Mirabella, M. "Feminist Self-Fashioning: Christine de Pizan and The Treasure of the City of Ladies." *European Journal of Women's Studies* 6 (1999): 9-20.

Berger, Harry, Jr. *Revisionary Play: Studies in the Spenserian Dynamics*. Berkeley, CA: University of California Press, 1988.

Blank, Paula. "The Proverbial 'Lesbian': Queering Etymology in Contemporary Critical Practice." *Modern Philology* 109, no. 1 (2011): 108-34.

Bloom, Harold. *The Anatomy of Influence*. New Haven, CT: Yale University Press, 2011.

The Anxiety of Influence: A Theory of Poetry. 2 ed. Oxford: Oxford University Press, 1997.

Brooks, Cleanth. *The Well-Wrought Urn: Studies in the Structure of Poetry*.

London: Methuen, 1968.

Burt, Richard. *Medieval and Early Modern Film and Media*. New York:

Palgrave, 2016.

Callaghan, Dympna. *Women and Gender in Renaissance Tragedy*. Harlow: Harvester Wheatsheaf, 1989.

Clark, Steve, and David Worrall, eds. *Historicising Blake*. New York: St. Martin's Press, 1994.

Daniell, David and Angus Easson. "Shakespeare." *The Year's Work in English Studies* 58:1 (1979): 127–171

DeCook, Travis, and Alan Galey, eds. *Shakespeare, the Bible, and the Form of the Book: Contested Scriptures*. London: Routledge, 2012.

Enterline, Lynn. *Shakespeare's Schoolroom: Rhetoric, Discipline, Emotion*. Philadelphia: University of Pennsylvania Press, 2012.

Foucault, Michel. *Surveiller et Punir: Naissance de la Prison* (Discipline and Punish: The Birth of the Prison). Translated by Alan Sheridan. London: Penguin, 1991.

Fowler, Alastair. *Spenser and the Numbers of Time*. London: Routledge, 1964.

Gallagher, Catherine, and Stephen Greenblatt. *Practicing New Historicism*. Chicago; London: University of Chicago Press, 2000.

Geertz, Clifford. *The Interpretation of Cultures*. 2nd ed. New York: Basic Books, 2000.

Goldberg, Jonathan. *Voice Terminal Echo*. New York: Methuen, 1986.

Greenblatt, Stephen. *Sir Walter Raleigh: The Renaissance Man and His Roles*. New Haven; London: Yale University Press, 1973.

ed. *The Power of Forms in the English Renaissance.* Norman, OK: Pilgrim Books, 1982.

"Resonance and Wonder." *Bulletin of the American Academy of Arts and Sciences* 43, no. 4 (1990): 11-34.

Will in the World: How Shakespeare Became Shakespeare. London: Random House, 2004.

Renaissance Self-Fashioning. 2nd ed. Chicago: University of Chicago Press, 2005.

The Swerve: How the Renaissance Began. London: Vintage, 2011.

Hadfield, Andrew. "The Relevance of Spenser." *Modern Philology* 106, no. 4 (2009): 686-701.

Howard, Jean E. "The Cultural Construction Of the Self in The Renaissance: Review of *Renaissance Self-Fashioning*." *Shakespeare Quarterly* 34, no. 3 (1983): 378-81.

The Stage and Social Struggle in Early Modern England. London: Routledge, 1994.

Hume, Robert D. "The Socio-Politics of London Comedy from Jonson to Steele." *Huntington Library Quarterly* 74, no. 2 (2011): 187-217.

Jardine, Lisa. "Strains of Renaissance Reading." *English Literary Renaissance* 25, no. 3 (1995): 289-306.

Kastan, David Scott. "Shakespeare After Theory." in *Opening The Borders:*

Inclusivity in Early Modern Studies ed. James V. Mirollo and Peter C. Herman. Newark, DE: University of Delaware Press, 2003: 206-225.

Keiser, Jess. "The Passion for the New." *Eighteenth-Century Studies*, 50:3

(2017), 337-340.

Leavis, F. R. *Revaluation: Tradition & Development in English Poetry.* London: Chatto & Windus, 1936.

McFaul, Tom. *Problem Fathers in Shakespeare and Renaissance Drama.* Cambridge: Cambridge University Press, 2012.

McGann, Jerome. "Keats and the Historical Method in Literary Criticism." *Modern Language Notes* 94, no. 5 (1979): 988-1032.

McManus, Clare. *Women on the Renaissance Stage: Anna of Denmark and Female Masquing in the Stuart Court (1590-1619).* Manchester: Manchester University Press, 2002.

Montrose, Louis Adrian. "The Elizabethan Subject and the Spenserian Text." In *Literary Theory / Renaissance Texts*, edited by Patricia Parker and David Quint. Baltimore: Johns Hopkins University Press, 1986.

"A Poetics of Renaissance Culture: Review of *Renaissance Self-Fashioning.*" *Criticism* 23, no. 4 (1981): 349-59.

The Subject of Elizabeth: Authority, Gender, and Representation. Chicago: University of Chicago Press, 2006.

Neely, Carol Thomas. "Constructing the Subject: Feminist Practice and the New Renaissance Discourses." *English Literary Renaissance* 18, no. 1 (Winter 1988): 5-18.

Orgel, Stephen. *The Illusion of Power: Political Theater in the English Renaissance.* Berkeley, CA: University of California Press, 1975.

Impersonations: The Performance of Gender in Shakespeare's England. Cambridge: Cambridge University Press, 1996.

Pechter, Edward. "The New Historicism and Its Discontents: Politicizing Renaissance Drama." *PMLA* 102 (1987): 292-303.

Quilligan, Maureen. "The Comedy of Female Authority in *The Faerie Queene.*" *English Literary Renaissance* 17 (1987): 156-71.

Gayatri Chakravorty Spivak, "The New Historicism: Political Commitment and the Post-modern critic" in *The New Historicism*, ed. Veeser, 277-93.

Tennenhouse, Leonard. "Strategies of State and Political Plays: *A Midsummer Night's Dream, Henry IV, Henry V, Henry VIII.*" In *Political Shakespeare*, edited by Jonathan Dollimore and Alan Sinfield. Manchester: Manchester University Press, 1994.

Thompson, E. P. *Witness Against the Beast*. Cambridge: Cambridge University Press, 1994.

Veeser, H. Aram. *The New Historicism*. London: Routledge, 2013.

Waller, Margaret. "Academic Tootsie: The Denial of Difference and the Difference It Makes: Review of *Renaissance Self-Fashioning*." *Diacritics* 17, no. 1 (1987): 2-20.

Webster, J. W. "Queering the Seventeenth Century: Historicism, Queer Theory, and Early Modern Literature." *Literature Compass*, 5 (2008): 376–393.

Woodbridge, Linda. *Women and the English Renaissance: Literature and the Nature of Womankind, 1540 to 1620*. Champaign, IL: University of Illinois Press, 1984.

Zammito, John H. "Are We Being Theoretical Yet? The New Historicism, the

New Philosophy of History, and 'Practicing Historians'." *The Journal of Modern History* 65, no. 4 (1993): 783-814.

THE MACAT LIBRARY
BY DISCIPLINE

The Macat Library By Discipline

AFRICANA STUDIES

Chinua Achebe's *An Image of Africa: Racism in Conrad's Heart of Darkness*
W. E. B. Du Bois's *The Souls of Black Folk*
Zora Neale Huston's *Characteristics of Negro Expression*
Martin Luther King Jr's *Why We Can't Wait*
Toni Morrison's *Playing in the Dark: Whiteness in the American Literary Imagination*

ANTHROPOLOGY

Arjun Appadurai's *Modernity at Large: Cultural Dimensions of Globalisation*
Philippe Ariès's *Centuries of Childhood*
Franz Boas's *Race, Language and Culture*
Kim Chan & Renée Mauborgne's *Blue Ocean Strategy*
Jared Diamond's *Guns, Germs & Steel: the Fate of Human Societies*
Jared Diamond's *Collapse: How Societies Choose to Fail or Survive*
E. E. Evans-Pritchard's *Witchcraft, Oracles and Magic Among the Azande*
James Ferguson's *The Anti-Politics Machine*
Clifford Geertz's *The Interpretation of Cultures*
David Graeber's *Debt: the First 5000 Years*
Karen Ho's *Liquidated: An Ethnography of Wall Street*
Geert Hofstede's *Culture's Consequences: Comparing Values, Behaviors, Institutes and Organizations across Nations*
Claude Lévi-Strauss's *Structural Anthropology*
Jay Macleod's *Ain't No Makin' It: Aspirations and Attainment in a Low-Income Neighborhood*
Saba Mahmood's *The Politics of Piety: The Islamic Revival and the Feminist Subject*
Marcel Mauss's *The Gift*

BUSINESS

Jean Lave & Etienne Wenger's *Situated Learning*
Theodore Levitt's *Marketing Myopia*
Burton G. Malkiel's *A Random Walk Down Wall Street*
Douglas McGregor's *The Human Side of Enterprise*
Michael Porter's *Competitive Strategy: Creating and Sustaining Superior Performance*
John Kotter's *Leading Change*
C. K. Prahalad & Gary Hamel's *The Core Competence of the Corporation*

CRIMINOLOGY

Michelle Alexander's *The New Jim Crow: Mass Incarceration in the Age of Colorblindness*
Michael R. Gottfredson & Travis Hirschi's *A General Theory of Crime*
Richard Herrnstein & Charles A. Murray's *The Bell Curve: Intelligence and Class Structure in American Life*
Elizabeth Loftus's *Eyewitness Testimony*
Jay Macleod's *Ain't No Makin' It: Aspirations and Attainment in a Low-Income Neighborhood*
Philip Zimbardo's *The Lucifer Effect*

ECONOMICS

Janet Abu-Lughod's *Before European Hegemony*
Ha-Joon Chang's *Kicking Away the Ladder*
David Brion Davis's *The Problem of Slavery in the Age of Revolution*
Milton Friedman's *The Role of Monetary Policy*
Milton Friedman's *Capitalism and Freedom*
David Graeber's *Debt: the First 5000 Years*
Friedrich Hayek's *The Road to Serfdom*
Karen Ho's *Liquidated: An Ethnography of Wall Street*

John Maynard Keynes's *The General Theory of Employment, Interest and Money*
Charles P. Kindleberger's *Manias, Panics and Crashes*
Robert Lucas's *Why Doesn't Capital Flow from Rich to Poor Countries?*
Burton G. Malkiel's *A Random Walk Down Wall Street*
Thomas Robert Malthus's *An Essay on the Principle of Population*
Karl Marx's *Capital*
Thomas Piketty's *Capital in the Twenty-First Century*
Amartya Sen's *Development as Freedom*
Adam Smith's *The Wealth of Nations*
Nassim Nicholas Taleb's *The Black Swan: The Impact of the Highly Improbable*
Amos Tversky's & Daniel Kahneman's *Judgment under Uncertainty: Heuristics and Biases*
Mahbub Ul Haq's *Reflections on Human Development*
Max Weber's *The Protestant Ethic and the Spirit of Capitalism*

FEMINISM AND GENDER STUDIES

Judith Butler's *Gender Trouble*
Simone De Beauvoir's *The Second Sex*
Michel Foucault's *History of Sexuality*
Betty Friedan's *The Feminine Mystique*
Saba Mahmood's *The Politics of Piety: The Islamic Revival and the Feminist Subject*
Joan Wallach Scott's *Gender and the Politics of History*
Mary Wollstonecraft's *A Vindication of the Rights of Woman*
Virginia Woolf's *A Room of One's Own*

GEOGRAPHY

The Brundtland Report's *Our Common Future*
Rachel Carson's *Silent Spring*
Charles Darwin's *On the Origin of Species*
James Ferguson's *The Anti-Politics Machine*
Jane Jacobs's *The Death and Life of Great American Cities*
James Lovelock's *Gaia: A New Look at Life on Earth*
Amartya Sen's *Development as Freedom*
Mathis Wackernagel & William Rees's *Our Ecological Footprint*

HISTORY

Janet Abu-Lughod's *Before European Hegemony*
Benedict Anderson's *Imagined Communities*
Bernard Bailyn's *The Ideological Origins of the American Revolution*
Hanna Batatu's *The Old Social Classes And The Revolutionary Movements Of Iraq*
Christopher Browning's *Ordinary Men: Reserve Police Batallion 101 and the Final Solution in Poland*
Edmund Burke's *Reflections on the Revolution in France*
William Cronon's *Nature's Metropolis: Chicago And The Great West*
Alfred W. Crosby's *The Columbian Exchange*
Hamid Dabashi's *Iran: A People Interrupted*
David Brion Davis's *The Problem of Slavery in the Age of Revolution*
Nathalie Zemon Davis's *The Return of Martin Guerre*
Jared Diamond's *Guns, Germs & Steel: the Fate of Human Societies*
Frank Dikotter's *Mao's Great Famine*
John W Dower's *War Without Mercy: Race And Power In The Pacific War*
W. E. B. Du Bois's *The Souls of Black Folk*
Richard J. Evans's *In Defence of History*
Lucien Febvre's *The Problem of Unbelief in the 16th Century*
Sheila Fitzpatrick's *Everyday Stalinism*

The Macat Library By Discipline

Eric Foner's *Reconstruction: America's Unfinished Revolution, 1863-1877*
Michel Foucault's *Discipline and Punish*
Michel Foucault's *History of Sexuality*
Francis Fukuyama's *The End of History and the Last Man*
John Lewis Gaddis's *We Now Know: Rethinking Cold War History*
Ernest Gellner's *Nations and Nationalism*
Eugene Genovese's *Roll, Jordan, Roll: The World the Slaves Made*
Carlo Ginzburg's *The Night Battles*
Daniel Goldhagen's *Hitler's Willing Executioners*
Jack Goldstone's *Revolution and Rebellion in the Early Modern World*
Antonio Gramsci's *The Prison Notebooks*
Alexander Hamilton, John Jay & James Madison's *The Federalist Papers*
Christopher Hill's *The World Turned Upside Down*
Carole Hillenbrand's *The Crusades: Islamic Perspectives*
Thomas Hobbes's *Leviathan*
Eric Hobsbawm's *The Age Of Revolution*
John A. Hobson's *Imperialism: A Study*
Albert Hourani's *History of the Arab Peoples*
Samuel P. Huntington's *The Clash of Civilizations and the Remaking of World Order*
C. L. R. James's *The Black Jacobins*
Tony Judt's *Postwar: A History of Europe Since 1945*
Ernst Kantorowicz's *The King's Two Bodies: A Study in Medieval Political Theology*
Paul Kennedy's *The Rise and Fall of the Great Powers*
Ian Kershaw's *The "Hitler Myth": Image and Reality in the Third Reich*
John Maynard Keynes's *The General Theory of Employment, Interest and Money*
Charles P. Kindleberger's *Manias, Panics and Crashes*
Martin Luther King Jr's *Why We Can't Wait*
Henry Kissinger's *World Order: Reflections on the Character of Nations and the Course of History*
Thomas Kuhn's *The Structure of Scientific Revolutions*
Georges Lefebvre's *The Coming of the French Revolution*
John Locke's *Two Treatises of Government*
Niccolò Machiavelli's *The Prince*
Thomas Robert Malthus's *An Essay on the Principle of Population*
Mahmood Mamdani's *Citizen and Subject: Contemporary Africa And The Legacy Of Late Colonialism*
Karl Marx's *Capital*
Stanley Milgram's *Obedience to Authority*
John Stuart Mill's *On Liberty*
Thomas Paine's *Common Sense*
Thomas Paine's *Rights of Man*
Geoffrey Parker's *Global Crisis: War, Climate Change and Catastrophe in the Seventeenth Century*
Jonathan Riley-Smith's *The First Crusade and the Idea of Crusading*
Jean-Jacques Rousseau's *The Social Contract*
Joan Wallach Scott's *Gender and the Politics of History*
Theda Skocpol's *States and Social Revolutions*
Adam Smith's *The Wealth of Nations*
Timothy Snyder's *Bloodlands: Europe Between Hitler and Stalin*
Sun Tzu's *The Art of War*
Keith Thomas's *Religion and the Decline of Magic*
Thucydides's *The History of the Peloponnesian War*
Frederick Jackson Turner's *The Significance of the Frontier in American History*
Odd Arne Westad's *The Global Cold War: Third World Interventions And The Making Of Our Times*

LITERATURE

Chinua Achebe's *An Image of Africa: Racism in Conrad's Heart of Darkness*
Roland Barthes's *Mythologies*
Homi K. Bhabha's *The Location of Culture*
Judith Butler's *Gender Trouble*
Simone De Beauvoir's *The Second Sex*
Ferdinand De Saussure's *Course in General Linguistics*
T. S. Eliot's *The Sacred Wood: Essays on Poetry and Criticism*
Zora Neale Huston's *Characteristics of Negro Expression*
Toni Morrison's *Playing in the Dark: Whiteness in the American Literary Imagination*
Edward Said's *Orientalism*
Gayatri Chakravorty Spivak's *Can the Subaltern Speak?*
Mary Wollstonecraft's *A Vindication of the Rights of Women*
Virginia Woolf's *A Room of One's Own*

PHILOSOPHY

Elizabeth Anscombe's *Modern Moral Philosophy*
Hannah Arendt's *The Human Condition*
Aristotle's *Metaphysics*
Aristotle's *Nicomachean Ethics*
Edmund Gettier's *Is Justified True Belief Knowledge?*
Georg Wilhelm Friedrich Hegel's *Phenomenology of Spirit*
David Hume's *Dialogues Concerning Natural Religion*
David Hume's *The Enquiry for Human Understanding*
Immanuel Kant's *Religion within the Boundaries of Mere Reason*
Immanuel Kant's *Critique of Pure Reason*
Søren Kierkegaard's *The Sickness Unto Death*
Søren Kierkegaard's *Fear and Trembling*
C. S. Lewis's *The Abolition of Man*
Alasdair MacIntyre's *After Virtue*
Marcus Aurelius's *Meditations*
Friedrich Nietzsche's *On the Genealogy of Morality*
Friedrich Nietzsche's *Beyond Good and Evil*
Plato's *Republic*
Plato's *Symposium*
Jean-Jacques Rousseau's *The Social Contract*
Gilbert Ryle's *The Concept of Mind*
Baruch Spinoza's *Ethics*
Sun Tzu's *The Art of War*
Ludwig Wittgenstein's *Philosophical Investigations*

POLITICS

Benedict Anderson's *Imagined Communities*
Aristotle's *Politics*
Bernard Bailyn's *The Ideological Origins of the American Revolution*
Edmund Burke's *Reflections on the Revolution in France*
John C. Calhoun's *A Disquisition on Government*
Ha-Joon Chang's *Kicking Away the Ladder*
Hamid Dabashi's *Iran: A People Interrupted*
Hamid Dabashi's *Theology of Discontent: The Ideological Foundation of the Islamic Revolution in Iran*
Robert Dahl's *Democracy and its Critics*
Robert Dahl's *Who Governs?*
David Brion Davis's *The Problem of Slavery in the Age of Revolution*

The Macat Library By Discipline

Alexis De Tocqueville's *Democracy in America*
James Ferguson's *The Anti-Politics Machine*
Frank Dikotter's *Mao's Great Famine*
Sheila Fitzpatrick's *Everyday Stalinism*
Eric Foner's *Reconstruction: America's Unfinished Revolution, 1863-1877*
Milton Friedman's *Capitalism and Freedom*
Francis Fukuyama's *The End of History and the Last Man*
John Lewis Gaddis's *We Now Know: Rethinking Cold War History*
Ernest Gellner's *Nations and Nationalism*
David Graeber's *Debt: the First 5000 Years*
Antonio Gramsci's *The Prison Notebooks*
Alexander Hamilton, John Jay & James Madison's *The Federalist Papers*
Friedrich Hayek's *The Road to Serfdom*
Christopher Hill's *The World Turned Upside Down*
Thomas Hobbes's *Leviathan*
John A. Hobson's *Imperialism: A Study*
Samuel P. Huntington's *The Clash of Civilizations and the Remaking of World Order*
Tony Judt's *Postwar: A History of Europe Since 1945*
David C. Kang's *China Rising: Peace, Power and Order in East Asia*
Paul Kennedy's *The Rise and Fall of Great Powers*
Robert Keohane's *After Hegemony*
Martin Luther King Jr.'s *Why We Can't Wait*
Henry Kissinger's *World Order: Reflections on the Character of Nations and the Course of History*
John Locke's *Two Treatises of Government*
Niccolò Machiavelli's *The Prince*
Thomas Robert Malthus's *An Essay on the Principle of Population*
Mahmood Mamdani's *Citizen and Subject: Contemporary Africa And The Legacy Of Late Colonialism*
Karl Marx's *Capital*
John Stuart Mill's *On Liberty*
John Stuart Mill's *Utilitarianism*
Hans Morgenthau's *Politics Among Nations*
Thomas Paine's *Common Sense*
Thomas Paine's *Rights of Man*
Thomas Piketty's *Capital in the Twenty-First Century*
Robert D. Putman's *Bowling Alone*
John Rawls's *Theory of Justice*
Jean-Jacques Rousseau's *The Social Contract*
Theda Skocpol's *States and Social Revolutions*
Adam Smith's *The Wealth of Nations*
Sun Tzu's *The Art of War*
Henry David Thoreau's *Civil Disobedience*
Thucydides's *The History of the Peloponnesian War*
Kenneth Waltz's *Theory of International Politics*
Max Weber's *Politics as a Vocation*
Odd Arne Westad's *The Global Cold War: Third World Interventions And The Making Of Our Times*

POSTCOLONIAL STUDIES

Roland Barthes's *Mythologies*
Frantz Fanon's *Black Skin, White Masks*
Homi K. Bhabha's *The Location of Culture*
Gustavo Gutiérrez's *A Theology of Liberation*
Edward Said's *Orientalism*
Gayatri Chakravorty Spivak's *Can the Subaltern Speak?*

PSYCHOLOGY

Gordon Allport's *The Nature of Prejudice*
Alan Baddeley & Graham Hitch's *Aggression: A Social Learning Analysis*
Albert Bandura's *Aggression: A Social Learning Analysis*
Leon Festinger's *A Theory of Cognitive Dissonance*
Sigmund Freud's *The Interpretation of Dreams*
Betty Friedan's *The Feminine Mystique*
Michael R. Gottfredson & Travis Hirschi's *A General Theory of Crime*
Eric Hoffer's *The True Believer: Thoughts on the Nature of Mass Movements*
William James's *Principles of Psychology*
Elizabeth Loftus's *Eyewitness Testimony*
A. H. Maslow's *A Theory of Human Motivation*
Stanley Milgram's *Obedience to Authority*
Steven Pinker's *The Better Angels of Our Nature*
Oliver Sacks's *The Man Who Mistook His Wife For a Hat*
Richard Thaler & Cass Sunstein's *Nudge: Improving Decisions About Health, Wealth and Happiness*
Amos Tversky's *Judgment under Uncertainty: Heuristics and Biases*
Philip Zimbardo's *The Lucifer Effect*

SCIENCE

Rachel Carson's *Silent Spring*
William Cronon's *Nature's Metropolis: Chicago And The Great West*
Alfred W. Crosby's *The Columbian Exchange*
Charles Darwin's *On the Origin of Species*
Richard Dawkin's *The Selfish Gene*
Thomas Kuhn's *The Structure of Scientific Revolutions*
Geoffrey Parker's *Global Crisis: War, Climate Change and Catastrophe in the Seventeenth Century*
Mathis Wackernagel & William Rees's *Our Ecological Footprint*

SOCIOLOGY

Michelle Alexander's *The New Jim Crow: Mass Incarceration in the Age of Colorblindness*
Gordon Allport's *The Nature of Prejudice*
Albert Bandura's *Aggression: A Social Learning Analysis*
Hanna Batatu's *The Old Social Classes And The Revolutionary Movements Of Iraq*
Ha-Joon Chang's *Kicking Away the Ladder*
W. E. B. Du Bois's *The Souls of Black Folk*
Émile Durkheim's *On Suicide*
Frantz Fanon's *Black Skin, White Masks*
Frantz Fanon's *The Wretched of the Earth*
Eric Foner's *Reconstruction: America's Unfinished Revolution, 1863-1877*
Eugene Genovese's *Roll, Jordan, Roll: The World the Slaves Made*
Jack Goldstone's *Revolution and Rebellion in the Early Modern World*
Antonio Gramsci's *The Prison Notebooks*
Richard Herrnstein & Charles A Murray's *The Bell Curve: Intelligence and Class Structure in American Life*
Eric Hoffer's *The True Believer: Thoughts on the Nature of Mass Movements*
Jane Jacobs's *The Death and Life of Great American Cities*
Robert Lucas's *Why Doesn't Capital Flow from Rich to Poor Countries?*
Jay Macleod's *Ain't No Makin' It: Aspirations and Attainment in a Low Income Neighborhood*
Elaine May's *Homeward Bound: American Families in the Cold War Era*
Douglas McGregor's *The Human Side of Enterprise*
C. Wright Mills's *The Sociological Imagination*

The Macat Library By Discipline

Thomas Piketty's *Capital in the Twenty-First Century*
Robert D. Putman's *Bowling Alone*
David Riesman's *The Lonely Crowd: A Study of the Changing American Character*
Edward Said's *Orientalism*
Joan Wallach Scott's *Gender and the Politics of History*
Theda Skocpol's *States and Social Revolutions*
Max Weber's *The Protestant Ethic and the Spirit of Capitalism*

THEOLOGY

Augustine's *Confessions*
Benedict's *Rule of St Benedict*
Gustavo Gutiérrez's *A Theology of Liberation*
Carole Hillenbrand's *The Crusades: Islamic Perspectives*
David Hume's *Dialogues Concerning Natural Religion*
Immanuel Kant's *Religion within the Boundaries of Mere Reason*
Ernst Kantorowicz's *The King's Two Bodies: A Study in Medieval Political Theology*
Søren Kierkegaard's *The Sickness Unto Death*
C. S. Lewis's *The Abolition of Man*
Saba Mahmood's *The Politics of Piety: The Islamic Revival and the Feminist Subject*
Baruch Spinoza's *Ethics*
Keith Thomas's *Religion and the Decline of Magic*

Macat Disciplines

*Access the greatest ideas and thinkers
across entire disciplines, including*

THE FUTURE OF DEMOCRACY

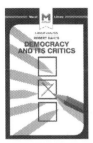   

Robert A. Dahl's, *Democracy and Its Critics*
Robert A. Dahl's, *Who Governs?*
Alexis De Toqueville's, *Democracy in America*
Niccolò Machiavelli's, *The Prince*
John Stuart Mill's, *On Liberty*
Robert D. Putnam's, *Bowling Alone*
Jean-Jacques Rousseau's, *The Social Contract*
Henry David Thoreau's, *Civil Disobedience*

Macat Disciplines

Access the greatest ideas and thinkers across entire disciplines, including

TOTALITARIANISM

Sheila Fitzpatrick's, *Everyday Stalinism*
Ian Kershaw's, *The "Hitler Myth"*
Timothy Snyder's, *Bloodlands*

Macat analyses are available from all good bookshops and libraries.

Access hundreds of analyses through one, multimedia tool.

Join free for one month **library.macat.com**

Printed in the United States
by Baker & Taylor Publisher Services